THE INSIDE ROOM

THE INSIDE ROOM

Eileen Mitson

Lakeland
Marshall Morgan & Scott
3 Beggarwood Lane, Basingstoke, Hants, RG23 7LP, UK

First published by Marshall Morgan & Scott in 1973
This edition re-issued in 1984

ISBN 0 551 01143 2

Printed in Great Britain by Cox & Wyman Ltd, Reading

To Arthur
whose love, for more than twenty years,
has enriched me beyond measure.

and

To Elizabeth
a daughter for whom I am
truly grateful.

With her, it was like there were two places—the inside room and the outside room ... The inside room was a very private place. She could be in the middle of a house full of people, and still feel like she was locked up by herself ...

The Heart is a Lonely Hunter
Carson McCullers

In every man there is a loneliness—an inner chamber of peculiar life into which God alone can enter ...

George Macdonald

Contents

	Introduction	9
1.	The Inner Chamber	15
2.	The Inner Image	29
3.	The Inner Flame	41
4.	The Inner Liberty	53
5.	The Inner Radiance	63
6.	The Inner Cry	73
7.	The Inner Rest	83
8.	The Inner Man—or Woman	95
9.	The Inner Eye	107
10.	The Inner Certainty	117

POEMS

The Dark and Lonely Place   13

In the Office Canteen   27

The Shape of Love   39

A Kind of Freedom   51

Invasion   61

Gifts   71

High Tide   81

Coming, Lads?   93

The Beginning of Wisdom   105

A Ballad of Life and Death   115

Introduction

It is odd how a phrase of music, a smell, or a familiar object can evoke certain memories with startling clarity, so that people, places and emotions are instantly called to mind. A certain rather ordinary bedside lamp, with a white, wooden base and a plain pink shade, will always be linked in my mind with the day I made a recording for the B.B.C.

Shortly before the publication of my book *Beyond the Shadows*, my publisher arranged for me to record an interview telling the story of my daughter Frankie for the radio programme 'Home this Afternoon'. We were in the throes of moving house at the time, as Arthur had been called to the pastorate of a Baptist church in Surrey, and on the way to the publisher's office I saw, in a small shop nearby, a table lamp which seemed to be exactly what we needed for our bedroom. I went into the shop, paid for the lamp, and arranged to pick it up after the interview was over.

But soon after I had been introduced to my interviewer, I was told that there was a taxi waiting outside, ready to take us to the recording studios in Piccadilly. Red-faced, I explained about the lamp waiting to be collected in a shop a couple of streets away.

'No trouble,' said my cheerful interviewer. 'Jump in the taxi, and we'll stop outside the shop so you can pick it up.'

And that is how, shortly afterwards, I arrived at the studios clutching under my arm an extremely bulky, awkward-shaped parcel which had to be left crouching clumsily by the microphone while the interview was being recorded. Often, when I switch on this lamp, I recall the odd mixture of dread and thrill which I felt at that moment as we waited for the recording light to go on: dread, because I was inwardly quailing at the thought of answering questions of such a personal nature over the air; and thrill, because I was equally certain that the whole thing was God's doing.

That lamp was, perhaps, symbolic of what was to follow. For from that day it was as if Frankie, and her simple story of suffering and triumph, was to light a lamp in the hearts of thousands of strangers all over the world: a lamp of hope.

Following the broadcast, I received a letter from Steve Race, who had compèred the programme and had introduced my talk. He enclosed several letters from listeners, and was kind enough to add a personal word of appreciation.

These letters were forerunners of a great many others which were to come my way during the following months, especially in the weeks immediately after the publication of the book.

It was thought, at first, that the story would be of help primarily to parents facing similar problems, and might therefore have a limited appeal. But it soon became apparent that this was not so. The first edition was sold out in a few months, and before long the book was published in the U.S.A. and several other countries.

It was the publishers of the German edition who predicted that it would be of value 'not only to parents who are being, or have been led, in similar paths, not only to those who are agonizing about the problem of suffering, but also those who question the reason for existence . . .'

Judging from the letters I have received from readers in various parts of the world, this is exactly the effect this straightforward story of God's dealings with an ordinary family has had. I have tried to answer all the letters received, as well as to fufil numerous requests to speak at meetings of one kind and another about the problem of suffering, and I feel that the many contacts made in this way have enriched me greatly. I have met some wonderful people, and been thrilled by many testimonies to God's keeping power in the dark experiences of life. Many have said that the book has helped them more than they can say, and I have had the joy of knowing that some have found Jesus Christ through reading it.

Often I have been asked: 'When are you going to write another book?' Although I now have six books in print, *Beyond the Shadows* has been the only one that is not fiction, and I know that the people who make inquiries about further works are hoping for something which will be in the nature of a follow-up for this story.

This book does not pretend to be quite that, but much that I have written in these pages has arisen from contacts made with my readers, whether by correspondence, or by personal encounter. Each chapter relates to some aspect of the inner life, and deals with the intensely personal nature of all spiritual experience. It is my prayer that this collection of meditations will be used to bring many more into closer contact with Jesus Christ, the Light of this dark world.

The Dark and Lonely Place

'Father!' He cried—for still the blessed bond
  United them; and the beloved Son
Was sheltered in the arms of Fatherhood . . .
  'I and my Father,' He had said, 'are one.'

'Forgive them, for they know not what they do!'
  They knew not—nor can mortals ever know
What Jesus knew, as there, upon the cross,
  He awaited the immortal hour of woe.

'My God, my God!' The dreadful hour is come!
  No longer 'Father,' but 'My God!' Well might
The noonday sun now hide her burning face
  And cloak the scene in simulated night!

'Why, why hast Thou forsaken Me?' He cried.
  Oh, that the Eternal Son, the Omniscient
In that dread moment should not comprehend
  Why from the Father's arms He must be rent!

Oh, dark unfathomable agony,
  Horror of sinfulness to sinlessness—
Not merely one man's sin, but all the world's
  Crushing the heart of Perfect Righteousness.

'Finished!' The word rings through the vault of heaven.
  Dawns the Eternal Day; the Night is o'er.
'Father, into Thy hands . . .' The Son of God
  Is clasped upon the Father's breast once more.

And can it be for me, my Saviour God,
*   You went into that dark and lonely place?*
Was it my shame my failure and my pride
*   That made the Father turn away His face?*

He bore my sin, my guilt, my punishment,
*   He was cut off, forsaken, cast aside,*
That I might never more forsaken be
*   But ever in the Father's love abide.*

1

The Inner Chamber

'What is the most devastating disease of today?' a doctor was recently asked.

'Loneliness,' he replied. 'Just plain loneliness.'

The problem of loneliness has come to the forefront in recent years to such an extent that no thinking person can fail to be concerned about it. Plays and novels have been written about it, radio and television have featured discussions about it, and social workers are constantly studying the various aspects of it. It is also interesting to note that the British Museum subject index now allocates to the subject of 'loneliness' a separate heading in the catalogue, where ten years ago it was completely ignored.

Francis Bacon, writing more than three hundred years ago, had this to say about the essential nature of loneliness:

'Little do men perceive what solitude is, and how far it extendeth. For a crowd is not company, and faces are but a gallery of pictures, and talk but a tinkling cymbal, where there is no love.'

A modern preacher endorsed this when he said that loneliness is a 'sense of unsatisfied desire. The lonely long for companionship, for friendship on an active basis. They long for that sense of completion and security that comes to those who feel they are wanted and cared for by others. They long to have contact with people, without feeling that they are a nuisance, or getting in the way. They long to feel that they are really doing something useful—that they would be missed if they were not there . . .'

Underneath all the mad, frenzied activity of the world around us, the getting and spending, the pleasure seeking, lies the basic need of the human spirit to find a purpose in life; a search, in fact, for identity. 'Who am I?' cries the awakening heart of the adolescent. The answer will work itself out only as he learns to relate and to adjust to those around him. And so it is for us all. We discover ourselves in those whom we love or hate: no man is an island. The man who strives to escape identification with another, who guards his independence jealously, is essentially an unhappy man, and he will be dogged all his life by loneliness. His outlook must eventually become warped, refracted, because he sees all things from the limited vantage point of his own ego.

It is, perhaps, this bid for independence which is at the root of much of the spiritual loneliness that has been described as the 'corroding ailment of the twentieth century'. Children are encouraged to think and act independently of adult control. Young people boast of their independence of all authority—whether it be parental, educational or religious. Women are asserting more strongly every day their independence of men in matters financial, emotional and physical. And men, for the most part, have always seemed to find it necessary to assert their independence of women.

The result is a world where every man, woman or child is so caught up with the business of fulfilling himself as an individual, that no-one has time, any more, for the one who needs him most. And if this need is denied, one may well ask, why should anyone bother? 'Everyone for himself' is the credo of our day. The result is widespread loneliness.

The truth is that God did not create us to be self-contained entities. No sooner had He created Adam, than He recognized the fact that 'it was not good for man to be alone'. Adam, we understand, was incomplete until God had created Eve. Whether they like it or not, men and women are still incomplete without each other. The family unit, with all its different parts interdependent upon each other, is a pattern created by God Himself; we try to change it at our peril. The relationship between husband and wife, parents and children is clearly set out for us both in the Old and New Testament, and the independence of the individual—whether male or female, old or young—is nowhere suggested.

Basically, of course, the essential individuality of each person is a real and vital fact. It is when we become unwilling or unable to communicate something of that individuality to others that the seeds of loneliness are sown. The Russian poet Tyutchev wrote:

> *Be silent, hide yourself, and let*
> *Your dreams and longing rise and set*

In the recesses of your heart . . .
How can the heart expression find,
Or one man read another's mind,
Another know what you live by?
A thought that's spoken is a lie . . .

The sensitive, contemplative spirit will have every sympathy with the sentiment expressed here. To what extent can we ever really communicate with another? 'A thought that's spoken is a lie'—not because we intend it to be, but because we can never give full expression to the complexity of thoughts and emotions which go to make up the essential 'I' which is at the core of each of us. There is a sense in which we must always remain strangers to our fellow-men.

The wife of Edward Thomas, the poet, underwent tremendous mental suffering because of her husband's periodic withdrawal from her. Although they were very close, with an intellectual affinity of which many might be envious, yet the melancholy nature of Thomas' temperament, combined with his masculine need for independence, caused him to go through periods of black despair. During these times, his wife's love and patience were an unspoken reproach to him, and he punished her for this with cruel words. Recording her feelings during one of these periods, Jenny wrote:

'I lie thinking of the strange bewilderment of things that is our life. I cannot understand it—birth, love, death—and all the different kinds of suffering; the loneliness of each one in spite of friendship, and love and sympathy—what can it mean?'

'What can it mean?' This, perhaps is the silent cry of our age. A cry to which, at times, there seems to be no answer. Any simple, or practical solutions offered to the problem, must of necessity seem inadequate in the face of the complex issues involved, and the best one can do is to make a few personal observations.

It seems to me that however poor a line of communication we may have between ourselves and those we love, it is vitally important that we do not allow this line to break. Today, there is so much superficiality in our living. For the most part, the conversation we make with each other is trivial. We carefully evade the main issues of life, fearful of 'getting out of our depth', or of betraying ourselves in some way. We do not, in fact, communicate. We simply talk. In the most voluble, outgoing, warm-hearted of family groups there may be those who are desperately lonely, hiding thoughts and feelings which they know would embarrass the others if they were to be expressed.

'But I had no idea how he was feeling! Why didn't he tell me?' cries the distraught parent who has dis-covered—through an outside agent, and often too late—of the deep trouble his child is in. At some point along the way, the precious line of communication has been broken.

Often in the case of the more reserved, inlooking child, the keeping of this line of communication open is a skilled and delicate task One needs to develop a sensitivity to the child's needs, carefully choosing the right time and place, and gently laying oneself open to shared confidences. Often one will be met with a rebuff—spoken or unspoken. This may be a clear indication that the moment chosen is the wrong one, but on no account should the parent give up, for deep in his heart this is the one thing the withdrawn child fears most.

The teen-age years are, perhaps, the most difficult, for this is when the desire for independence is at its strongest. Some young people develop and mature at an alarming rate during these years—not only physically, but mentally too. Many a parent has woken up one morning to find in place of a lovable, high spirited child, a morose and prickly stranger. Clashes of will, and outbursts of temperament on both sides do little to help the situation.

It is a lamentable fact of life that we so easily forget that period of our own adolescence, so that when we are con-fronted with the signs of similar adjustment in our children, we find it difficult to be patient and understanding.

'I'm sure I was never like that,' we say with exasperation, when a little honest thinking will remind us that we were probably worse. If we do get to the point of admitting this, then we will probably try to justify ourselves by saying: 'But for me it was different. My parents just didn't try to understand . . .' (The truth is that we find it virtually impos-sible to view objectively any situation in which we our-selves are involved. It is as though there is a mechanical device which automatically drops a blindfold over the eyes of the ego whenever a mirror is approached. This device is, of course, the cause of most of the world's ills.)

Many young people go through extreme mental anguish during the formative years, and their resultant behaviour can be such that everyone—not least they themselves—is baffled. A young man in trouble with the authorities gave as his reason for his offence: 'Because I was lonely.' How often do we hear of young people who say: 'My parents don't care what happens to me. They're too busy with their own affairs.' Often, it must be admitted, in these days of material-ism, pleasure seeking and self-fulfilment, this is true. But just as often the truth is that the parents do care. They care desperately. But they feel incapable of showing it, of putting their love into words or actions. Often there are barriers to communication which cannot be destroyed overnight, be-cause they have been built brick by brick over years of secret emotional conflict. Self-doubt, wounded pride, fear, prejudice or guilt may have gone into the building of such barriers. In such cases the solution must lie, initially, in the taking off of blindfolds.

The tragic lack of understanding which can exist between the younger and older generations was depicted in a tele-vision production not long ago, in which parents and offspring are seen confronting each other in hopeless silence. The parents are thinking: 'If only she'd talk to me, I'd try to understand,' while the teen-ager is thinking: 'If I thought they'd listen, I'd talk to them.' There is, surely, a profound lesson somewhere here.

If the line of communication is easily broken between parent and child, it is, sadly, just as easily broken between husband and wife, as the present day rate of divorce shows all too clearly. In the early days of courtship and marriage, young people talk with comparative ease about their inner feelings, their hopes and their fears. But so complex and primitive a bond is that between a man and a woman, that this free intercourse of spirit with spirit soon becomes coloured by attitudes and reactions almost too deep-rooted for analysis.

The first thing that happens to most young married couples is that an element of disillusionment sets in. The young man finds that the gentle, attractive and adoring girl he married can be unpredictable, unreasonable and critical. What is more, the criticism is sometimes levelled at himself; and this, when he had expected unqualified admiration, is a severe blow to his ego. Instead of admitting to himself—and to her—that he *needs* her love and devotion, he behaves as though he had a right to it. Similarly, the girl may find that the handsome, chivalrous and noble man she married thinks nothing, a few years later, of sitting with his feet up after Sunday lunch, while she struggles to cope, alone, with a mountain of greasy dishes and three fractious toddlers. And rarely, now, does he take her in his arms outside the bedroom. Her desire to be loved and cherished *for what she is*, and not for what she can give, is deeply wounded. If she reacts, she will do so indirectly: and many a nagging woman hides in her heart a deep, inexpressible hurt.

It is these kinds of hurt—the ones which strike at the root of our basic human nature—which often cause a build-up of disappointment, resentment and even bitterness in a normal marriage relationship. It is because husband and wife are each, in their own way, so vulnerable to hurt from the other, that real communication becomes so difficult. Both go into marriage fondly believing that they love the other more than anything on earth, and rarely getting around to the stark truth that it is themselves they really love most in the final analysis. To fuse one's life with that of another is often a painful process. It calls for a great deal of self-denial and humility, and this is perhaps why so few marriages are truly successful.

Perhaps the loneliest people of all are those who are partners of an unhappy marriage. For what can be more poignantly heartbreaking than the continued physical union of two people whose spirits have given up all hope of being united? Just as one feels lonelier in a crowd than on a mountain top, so the partner of an unhappy marriage relationship can feel more starkly lonely than the single person who lives alone. The despairing *cri de coeur*: 'I can't get through to him any more!' is followed all too quickly by its hollow echo: 'And I never shall again!' After twenty, thirty or forty years of married life, few situations can be more heart-rending than the one which finds husband and wife confronting each other at the breakfast table as perfect strangers. The line of communication is irretrievably broken.

Once more, the only answer to this problem is a preventative one. However hard it may be, in the early years of marriage, to keep the lines open, it must be regarded as the most important aspect of marriage. The line of communication is indeed a life-line. For the most part, women find it easier to talk about their inner feelings than men do. The husband who has something on his mind will often respond with a curt rebuff to the wife who tries to coax him to 'talk about it'. A wife, on the other hand, usually feels a sense of compulsion when it comes to pouring out her troubles! She longs to unburden herself, to talk it out, and if, as sadly often happens, her husband is unwilling to lend a sympathetic ear, then she will often turn to her mother, or a close friend. This, of course, may widen the gap between husband and wife, for her troubles often revolve around her relationship with *him*—the root reason for his unwillingness to listen in the first place. Again his basic fear of being found wanting makes him shy away from communication on this level. Women, perhaps, are slow to understand how deeply important it is for a man to believe in himself. Many marriages break down because of a general lack of understanding about the basic differences of the sexes.

A marriage partnership where there is close communion between husband and wife at every level, where there are no secrets, and where no misunderstandings are allowed to thrive, is the most precious relationship on earth. I would add humbly, that I speak from experience. Just after the death of our daughter, someone said to me: 'Can you think of any experience which would have been more bitter?' My reply was: 'Yes. To have faced it alone.' What I meant was not simply to have faced the experience as one person on my own, but to have faced it without the love, support and close harmony of our deeply happy marriage.

I have heard of marriages being saved by shared trouble, but I have also heard of relationships which have suffered a fatal blow in just such circumstances as those that we passed through. This to me, must be the ultimate suffering. In reviewing *Beyond the Shadows*, someone paid tribute to my husband in this way: 'He provides the key to the regenerative quality of married love which can redeem any tragedy: as together they faced the imminent death of their child, he took his wife in his arms and whispered, "I love you, darling—I love you".'

Married love is regenerative only when the line of communication is kept open, and this quotation from my story mentioned above perhaps serves to illustrate this profound truth. When we clung to each other, whispering of love, we were communicating to each other all that our lips could not find words for in that moment of stark tragedy. If the happiness of marriage depended on our being able to express eloquently all that was in our hearts at all times, none would succeed. A touch of the hand, a look in the eye, or a simple demonstration of love can all speak clearly to the beloved. He will understand, though no words have been spoken aloud. The ultimate physical expression of love between husband and wife can, and often does, speak volumes. But only if it is the physical expression of an established harmony, a sacrament of self-giving, not just an exercise in mutual self-indulgence.

So far I have written of loneliness only in the context of the family—the setting in which, perhaps, one least expects to find it. But the same principles apply to those who are not blessed with family ties, for every man is essentially alone, and will find fulfilment only in others. Some of the loveliest relationships exist between those individuals who do not fit in with any particular family circle. The single person, or the one who has lost a life-partner, only discovers himself anew in the relationships he forms with others. He learns to give himself, to be outgoing, to recognize that loneliness can be a self-inflicted disease. Love, on any level, is ninety per cent giving, and only as we open our hearts to the needs of others shall we find balm for the hurt and loneliness that we keep hidden there.

On the other hand there are many lonely people whose lives could be transformed by a little more thoughtfulness, a little less self-centredness on the part of the rest of us. Sometimes all that is needed is a few moments of our time spent in chatting over the garden wall, or in the street. Often, a few hours spent regularly each week with an elderly person who knows we can be relied upon to send a message if we are unable to come, can mean more than words can tell. As has already been observed, to know that *somebody cares* is the basic need of the human soul.

In the last analysis, it must be said again that there is a core of loneliness in every human being who walks the earth, no matter how close and communicative a relationship he may enjoy with another person. George MacDonald, Victorian novelist and poet said: 'In every man there is a loneliness—an inner chamber of peculiar life into which God alone can enter.' This basic loneliness from which we all suffer is essentially a spiritual loneliness.

In *The Heart is a Lonely Hunter* a modern American novelist expressed the deep sense of isolation experienced by the main character like this: 'She went into the inside room. With her it was like there were two places—the inside room and the outside room . . . The inside room was a very private place. She could be in the middle of a house full of people, and still feel like she was locked up by herself . . .'

We each of us have an inside room in which we are locked up by ourselves. Yet God waits to enter this inner chamber—your 'inside room' and mine. This was the whole purpose of Christ's coming. By nature we are alienated not only from God and from others, but from ourselves. We are fragmented, incomplete, lost and confused. Our inside room is in darkness. In Holman Hunt's famous picture 'The Light of the World', Christ is depicted outside a door holding a lamp. The idea is based on Revelation chapter 3 verse 20: 'Behold I stand at the door and knock. If any man hear my voice and open the door, I will come in and sup with him and He with me.' 'Christ in you,' said Paul—'the hope of glory!'

This is the ultimate in communication, because the relationship between a man and his God is the only one in which there are no secrets whatever. As David said: 'O, Lord, thou hast searched me and known me. Thou knowest my downsitting and mine uprising, thou understandest my thoughts afar off . . .' In face of this awful knowledge, David felt compelled to cry out: 'Whither shall I go then, from Thy presence?' Comforting though it may be to know that God understands us through and through, it is also terrifying, for none of us dare stand before God almighty in a state of spiritual nakedness.

No, we dare not approach and expose ourselves to His all-seeing gaze, but when it is the nail-pierced hand of Christ which knocks upon the door of our inside room, and bids us open up to Him, then that is a different matter. Because those nail-prints are a token for us of the fact that He has taken upon Himself the burden of our sin and unworthiness. By His death on the cross, He has broken down 'the middle wall of partition' between us and God. He was, as it were, alienated from His Father at Calvary, that we might be reconciled, made whole. Once we accept this by faith, there is nothing to keep Him out of the 'inside room'.

This is the answer to the fundamental loneliness which

lies hidden in the heart of every man. Jesus says, 'If any man hear my voice and open the door ...' To His disciples He said: 'If a man love me, he will keep my words and my Father will love him, and we will come unto him and make our abode with him.'

Once you open the door of your 'inside room' to Him, you can never be truly alone again.

O, Jesus Christ, Light of the world, and Saviour of mankind

Help me, now, to listen for the sound of Your knock on my heart's door.

Help me to understand that when You went into that dark and lonely place,

That place of separation from the Father's love,

You went there for me: that I might never again suffer the anguish of alienation, the pain of loneliness.

O, Blessed Lord, come in, and bring Your Light into my inside room;

Dispelling the darkness, the fear, the failure;

Come, sit with me, and sup with me.

For in Your love, I am made whole. I am reconciled, I am complete.

Hand in hand with You, I can face the world, I can go out and give myself to others, I can create happiness wherever I go.

And help me, Lord, to remember, that You have set the solitary in families,

That we are members one of another,

That no man lives unto himself,

That I need my fellow man, and he needs me.

May I never shut out from my heart's fire

Any who would warm themselves there.

May I never hold back from speaking the word

Or giving the touch, or the look

Which will help a man to escape from the prison of himself,

And make him know that he is loved.

Amen

In the Office Canteen

I looked, and thought I knew them all—
  Some proudly short, some meekly tall;
When, suddenly, as I stood there
  My dreaming gaze became a stare—
For all their masks fell off.

And underneath, I saw—I saw—
  Their naked souls. I looked no more;
The room grew cold, that summer's day—
  I thought, before I turned away:
They're strangers, every one!

And then, upon the further wall,
  Behind the steaming coffee stall,
I saw my own face in a glass
  Bland, void, the eyes expressionless:
And I cried: Who am I?

2
The Inner Image

One of the words which has taken on a new significance in recent years, appearing with a certain regularity in the writings of modern thinkers, playwrights and novelists is the word 'identity'. Who am I, really, underneath the face that I wear, underneath the words that I say, underneath the mechanism of the life that I live? What meaning, if any, has the 'I' which crouches at the centre of my being? Can I ever understand myself, let alone hope to be understood by others?

We have already considered the difficulties of communication, and the way in which we, as individuals, discover ourselves only when we are able to give ourselves in love for another. C. S. Lewis wrote a novel in which he re-interpreted the love story of Cupid and Psyche, and he called his story *Till We Have Faces*. The central character is an ugly, unhappy woman who has a deep, fierce love for her beautiful younger sister. Although she thinks she understands her own love, and her own consequent actions and motives so well, there comes a time when she is forced to see herself as she really is. Her face, which she usually covers with a veil, is made bare.

'Lightly men talk of saying what they mean . . .' she says. 'When the time comes to you at which you will be forced at last to utter the speech which has lain at the centre of your soul for years . . . you'll not talk about the joy of words. I saw well why the gods do not speak to us openly, nor let us answer. Till that word can be dug out of us, why should they hear the babble that we think we mean? How can they meet us face to face *till we have faces?*'

God is concerned with our true identity, and with nothing else. Until we are ready to be unveiled before Him, we can have no dealings with Him. Nor can we come to terms with our own selves, our own individuality, the purpose which God has for the 'I' that is at the core of us. But we shrink from having those faces unveiled.

The human face is that part of us which gives us our

individuality. Of all the millions of human beings who inhabit our earth, no two of them are alike. Even so-called 'identical' twins have their distinguishing features, for those who know them best can recognize them immediately by the personality which registers itself so clearly on their countenance. It is, then, our personality which gives us that 'look' which is exclusively ours. That is why, when we look at the face of the dead, we say with such conviction: 'He is not there.' The body is but a shell, the face itself bears now little resemblance to the face we loved, because the person who inhabited it has gone.

No other part of our bodies have the same significance as our faces. The young wife who blurted out to the marriage guidance counsellor: 'He never touches my face!' was giving expression to a deep-rooted human emotion. *What we are* matters to us desperately, and we want, above all, to know that it matters to those whom we love. This woman, haunted by the fear that she herself was unlovable, had come to dread the physical aspects of her marriage because she felt de-personalized, a mere 'faceless' source of satisfaction for the man she loved.

In a private collection of Victorian dolls, there is one with an unusual head. Swivel it round inside its bonnet, and you will discover three different faces—or rather, the same face wearing three different expressions. In a way, we are like that three-faced doll; for it might be said that we, too, have three faces: there is the face the world sees; the face we see ourselves; and the face God sees.

We care what our physical faces look like. Many women will not venture out in public until they have 'put a face on'. Uncertain of the one with which nature has endowed them, they make a mask and wear that instead! We care even more what kind of an image we present to the outside world. We want to be admired, perhaps, but we want, most of all to be liked.

David was greatly admired. He was good looking, had red cheeks and bright eyes. He was a shepherd, gentle by nature, yet fearless enough to tackle a lion and a bear single-handed when they threatened his flock. He was a poet and a musician, and had all the qualities one might most admire in a man. Yet it was not his qualities alone—and certainly not his good looks—for which God selected him to be king over Israel. 'Man looketh on the outward appearance,' said

Samuel, 'but God looks on the heart.' God chose David, not for any attributes that he might have had, but because of what he was, and what, under God, he could be.

All the same, it was for his attributes that men admired David, as men always will. When he killed the giant Goliath, then he became a real hero. People sang his praises. 'Saul has killed his thousands, but David his tens of thousands,' they jubilated. Physical courage is always admired—even when it is coupled with arrogance. But David was calm and unassuming. He was mighty, but he was cool with it. Certainly, he was not only admired, but he was liked.

But was this 'face' of David, the one the world saw, his true 'face'? How many people really understood the essential man that was David? How many could have known that underneath the soldier's armour lay a sensitive, poet's heart, tender and vulnerable as a woman's?

And how often do we stop to think that underneath the smiling, self-confident exterior of our neighbour's face may lie a lonely, uncertain or fearful heart? When we move among others, putting on a 'good face' to cover our shyness or our self-doubt, we rarely stop to think that the people we fear so much may, in fact, be terrified of us! We have grown accustomed to taking people at their 'face value'.

We have only to think about people who are constantly in the public eye to realize how true this is. The personality projected upon the television screen, for example, often bears no resemblance to the character who is actually behind the public figure. We have all been surprised, at some time or another, to read about the private life of someone we have admired for years. We may even feel let down, betrayed, unable to believe what is written in the newspaper report. It is, in fact, pretty terrifying to realize how little we know about the man we travel to town with every day, or the woman who works beside us at the factory bench. What sorrows, what heart-aches, what virtues or vices our public faces often hide!

People have been known to wake up one morning to find that their next door neighbour is an enemy agent, or that the man they play golf with every Saturday morning is a murderer, or a bank robber. Conversely, we may discover that the terse, unsmiling character whom we have always done our best to avoid, has, in fact, a heart of gold and is loved by all who take the trouble to get under his skin. Or the woman who works in our local wool-shop, and who always seems to be on top of things, always smiling and ready with a joke, may, in fact be carrying a tremendous burden: she may have an invalid husband, or a wayward child at home.

The face we show the world is not always our true face. Often it is the face we make ourselves, a mask intended to represent the sort of people we would like to be. Or it may be a mask which some deep-rooted reserve makes us wear in order to discourage others from getting too close to us. Even those who are closest to us do not really know us as we are. There is a sense in which the world is one vast 'strangers' gallery', each man having locked deep within him—in a place which he himself cannot reach—the secret of his true identity.

To speak, then of deliberately hiding our true identity from others will not really do, because the trouble is that we are strangers not only to others, but also to ourselves. The face we see ourselves, though we might expect it to be our true face, is often as false as the one we show the world. For if it is important that we appear attractive to others, it is even more important that we appear attractive to ourselves. It is desperately important to us that we are able to respect ourselves. Perhaps this is why other people often see the faults which we ourselves are blind to. The truth is that we do not want to see them. We are as careful about the face we show ourselves as we are about the face we show the world.

How did David see himself that day as he sat upon the roof top and saw Bathsheba bathing? As a king, worshipped by all, admired, respected? A man who could do no wrong? A man set apart for special privileges? In that moment of strong physical temptation, David was aware of only one thing: 'I want her. (After all, I'm a king: I can have what I like.) I must have her. (After all, I'm only human.)'

Satan is very clever with his blindfold. He makes sure we do not catch a glimpse of our real faces in moments like these. He gets at us through our baser natures—if not through lust, then through pride, self-love, greed or jealousy.

'Why should I be a doormat?' we ask ourselves as we hear the bitter, angry words issuing forth from our own mouths. Hurtful words, repaying blow for blow. 'Why shouldn't I have it?' we say peevishly, as we help ourselves to something which, in the hands of a more needy brother would have lightened his heavy load. 'Why should she have everything?' snaps jealousy, with tongue as quick and sharp as a knife. The very fact that we ask these questions shows that we have already had a glimpse of our real faces. But we cover them up quickly, because we do not like what we see. And desperately we look for justification for what is already done.

James said that we are like a man who beholds his natural face in a mirror and straightway goes away and forgets what manner of man he is. The Word of God is the mirror, for when we read it, the Holy Spirit shows us ourselves as we really are. But we do not honestly want to know. The revelation is too uncomfortable, too disturbing. 'The heart of man,' said an Old Testament writer, 'is deceitful above all things, and desperately wicked. Who can know it?' Who, indeed? Not we ourselves, it seems.

I was introduced to a woman whom, I was assured, everybody liked. I could see why. She was friendly, humorous, warm, lively. Her face was a pleasure to look at. She had, I suppose, what is described as an 'attractive personality'. Yet I discovered later that this woman had borne a grudge against her own brother for seven years, and had not once spoken to him in all that time. I knew what kind of face she presented to the world. But what kind of face did she present to herself? The truth is that we all protect ourselves fiercely from the knowledge of what we really are. And in doing so, we rob ourselves of true identity.

'Behold', cried David, in his great psalm of confession, 'thou desirest truth in the inward parts: and in the hidden part thou shalt make me to know wisdom.'

So the masks we wear are really for a defence—a defence against the knowledge of others, a defence against our own knowledge. But there is no defence against the knowledge of God. 'Through every mask,' wrote Karl Barth, 'God sees the real faces of men.' David knew this when he wrote the 139th psalm:

> O, Lord, thou has searched me and known me
> Thou knowest my downsitting and my uprising,
> Thou understandest my thought afar off.
> Thou compassest my path and my lying down
> And art acquainted with all my ways . . .

Such knowledge is too wonderful for me.
It is high, I cannot attain to it . . .

In this psalm, the wonder of God's love comes through to us like a ray of warm sunshine. We pause in our flight from Him and cautiously draw back the veil from our faces. Can it be—is it possible—that the God who knows us so thoroughly actually loves us?

God had known what was in David's heart from the very beginning. He knew about the victories, and He knew about the failures. He knew about the sin, and He knew about the heartache. But God chose him just the same. It would be of little comfort to know that God sees right into the heart, into the hidden parts, the parts which are hidden even from our own eyes, if we did not believe that God loves us in spite of what we are.

There is a legend which tells of how Adam said to the angel who guarded the gate of Eden: 'What shall I bring back so that you will let me in again?' Came the answer from the angel: 'Bring back the face God first gave you.'

For the faces which God gave us in the beginning were beautiful, unmarred by rebellion and sin. We were banished from the garden of God's presence because He could no longer look upon us. Well might Adam and Eve hang their heads in shame when the angel said there would be no re-entry to the garden until they had again found those faces, had won back the beauty first given them at the beginning of time! How could they? What could they do to change what they had wilfully ruined?

In the story told by C. S. Lewis—a myth, of course, but with a Christian message—the unhappy, ugly heroine was at last brought face to face with her own spiritual nakedness, her 'facelessness'. Standing by the edge of a pool with Psyche, her beautiful sister, she awaits with terror the judgment of the great God of the Mountain. But it is when we are ready for judgment that Love takes us by surprise. This is what actually happened:

'The air was growing brighter and brighter about us; as if something had set it on fire. Each breath I drew let into me new terror, joy, overpowering sweetness. I was pierced through and through with the arrows of it. *I was being unmade.* I was no one . . .'

And then she sees, reflected in the water at their feet, two faces, one her own, one Psyche's. But what is this? What has happened? For both faces are beautiful! Her ugliness has been destroyed. She has been re-created. In her 'unmaking', she is re-made.

Can we ever take back to the garden of God's presence the face of beauty He first gave us? The wonder of it is that we can. There is a price to be paid, but we are not the ones who must pay it. Love pays the price: we can have nothing to do with it. We must, however, be brought to the point where we are willing to be 'unmade'. We must be ready to see ourselves as we really are—marred, imperfect, unfit for the garden—and then we must be willing to accept a beauty that is not our own, that is not of our making. But what is the price, and who pays it?

Oscar Wilde wrote an allegory about a young man obsessed by his own beauty. When Dorian Gray saw that beauty being transferred to a canvas by an artist friend of his, the thought came to him that there was no way by which he could hold on to his good looks. He knew that one day he would be old and ugly, marred not only by the passage of the years, but the imperfections of his own character. He longed with all his heart that this might not be so—and his wish was granted. From that time on it was the painting which grew old and withered with the years; he himself remained as he had been at the time it was painted—fresh with the bloom of youth.

As time went by, Dorian Gray became more and more corrupt, indulging all the fleshly appetites; he was vain, arrogant, selfish and greedy. Yet none of these corrupting forces showed in his face because of the terrible wish he had been granted. People envied him for his good looks, his continuing youthfulness. But the day came when Dorian Gray began to be haunted by the thought of the hideous portrait hidden away in the attic, and in bitter remorse, he killed the artist who painted it. Then he went again to look at the portrait, vowing to turn over a new leaf, vowing to lead a good life.

'Perhaps if his life became pure, he would be able to expel every sign of evil passion from the face. Perhaps the signs of evil had already gone away. He would go and look. He took the lamp from the table and crept upstairs. As he unbarred the door, a smile of joy flitted across his strangely young-looking face ... yes, he would be good, and the hideous thing that he had hidden away would no longer be a terror to him. He felt as if the load had been lifted from him already.'

But when he finally lifted the veil from the picture, he was appalled to see that there was no improvement whatsoever, 'save that in the eyes there was a look of cunning, and in the mouth the curved wrinkle of the hypocrite. The thing was still loathsome, more loathsome if possible, than before.'

Those who know the story will be familiar with its ending. Dorian Gray, in deep despair, takes a knife and slashes the offending portrait in an anguished attempt to destroy it. Below, walking in the street, two men hear a horrible cry issuing from the attic above, and rush up the stairs to see who has been hurt. On the wall they find a splendid portrait of Dorian Gray as they last saw him, but lying on the floor, with a knife in his heart, is a withered, wrinkled and loathsome old man.

There is a grim lesson in this story, for we are each of us making a 'face' for our own souls each day. No matter what kind of 'face' we present to the outside world, only God sees our true face. We may, like Dorian Gray, be able to deceive both ourselves and others, but we can never deceive God. In the light of His holiness and purity the 'face' of humankind is loathsome to behold, and there is nothing we can do to change it.

But there is another lesson, too, to be extracted from Oscar Wilde's story. For the wonder of it is that God Himself has provided the answer to our dilemma. He offers us His beauty, and He Himself pays the price, for He is Love. Isaiah, in foretelling the great act of redemption, says: 'His visage was marred more than any man's.'

Jesus Christ, the Son of God, took upon Himself our ugliness, that we might be partakers of the divine nature, the divine beauty.

'There was no beauty,' says Isaiah, 'that we should desire Him.'

They spat upon His face, they plucked out the hair, they pressed a crown of thorns upon His lovely brow. The face that had glowed with love for all humanity, the face that had shone with the glory of God on the Mount of Transfiguration, was marred beyond recognition.

This is the price He paid. Like the beautiful portrait which took upon itself the ugliness and loathsomeness of Dorian Gray, so the divine nature took upon itself the deformity of the human race. We tried to destroy Him for it, but true beauty is indestructible. Love is eternal.

When we stand at the gate of heaven, at the gate of the garden of God's presence, we shall present to Him not our own beauty, but His. For 'we, beholding as in a glass the glory of the Lord, are changed into the same image, from glory unto glory.'

In Christ alone we find our true identity.

O, Jesus Christ, my Lord,
   I need not begin by explaining myself to You
   Because You have been a man, and You know what is in
      man.
   You looked beyond the face of the rich young ruler,
   You saw what he lacked, yet You loved him;
   And, underneath the friendly face of the woman of Sam-
      aria,
   You saw the sin and the yearning;
   When Nicodemus showed You his respectable, respectful
      face,
   You saw the heart need which he was afraid to show.
   And, Saviour of mankind, I do not need to explain myself
      to you.
   For You know me through and through.
   You know when I get up and you know when I sit
      down
   You know what I am thinking before the thoughts are
      properly formed;
   You know all about the loneliness;
   You know my heart's yearning for a fuller, richer life;
   You know how often I fail in the battle against evil;
   You see the tears I shed in secret,
   The frustration, and the questing after answers which
      always seem to elude me;
   You know how I long for fulfilment;
   How I long to know that there is a purpose in life—
   A purpose and a meaning for me . . .
   And so, Lord, I just ask that You will take me,
   Unmake me, and then re-make me
   In Your image;
   That You will empty my poor heart of all its treasured
      trash
   And fill it with the riches of Your precious love.
   For in You, and You only
   I am alive,
   I am real,
   I have purpose,
   And I have meaning.
   So take me, Lord.
   I am ready, now, to be born.

                                                    Amen

The Shape of Love

The shape of love
is the shape of a cross:
for love is self-giving.

Love is the place
where, among the dead,
we find the living.

In love we die daily,
gladly, to self—
find regeneration:

For in love we awake
with a name and a face—
a new creation.

3
The Inner Flame

Perhaps the most overworked, abused little word in our English language is the four-lettered word 'love'.

'What the world needs today,' say the idealists, 'is LOVE'. Our first re-action to this observation is to nod our heads in vigorous agreement. Of course, of course—love is the answer: love for our neighbour, love for our coloured brothers and sisters, love for the starving millions of Asia, love for the drug addict, the dropout, the outcasts of society. If only, *if only* we could all love each other, what a marvellous place this world would be. Love is the panacea offered for all our ills. And of course, it *is* the answer—if only we really knew what the word meant.

An Englishman may speak of his love for steak and chips, or for his children, or he may speak of making love to his wife, or of the love of God, and he will use the same word in every case. The Greeks were more discriminating—they had four words for love. *Eros* means the love of a man for a woman. It includes an element of physical passion, and is never used in the New Testament at all. *Philia* is the warm love which we feel for a close friend, and involves the feelings of the heart; *storge* implies the kind of affection which parents feel for their children; and *agape* is an essentially Christian word, meaning sacrificial, giving love—the kind of love which stems not only from the heart and the feelings, but from the mind.

It is surely this last kind of love, the *agape* of the New Testament, that the world really needs. Once we realize what we are really saying when we speak so glibly of love, then we may well draw back a little. For let us make no mistake about it—this kind of love is going to make demands upon us. True love is not merely a surge of sympathetic emotion which we can direct at anybody who seems in need of affection. This an an easy exercise, but sadly futile.

Human relationships are breaking down all around us because we have never properly understood that love means self-giving, and involves the will and the mind. 'Love seeks not her own,' Paul reminds us in his famous letter on love, and here, surely we come to the heart of the matter. In every kind of relationship, whether it be that of nation with nation, man with man, husband with wife, parents with child, friend with friend, brother with sister, or whatever it may be, it is the element of self-seeking which is the canker at the core of things.

This, of course, is why God sent His Son to earth. One of the shortest, best known texts in the Bible, one which we learned as little children, almost as soon as we could speak, is John's profound assertion that 'God is Love'. But almost as well-known are the words with which John amplifies this 'God so loved the world that *He gave* . . .' He gave Himself. He gave His only begotten Son. This is the essence of love: self-giving. We might say that love is cross-shaped, for there is no true love without sacrifice, no sacrifice without love.

Not only did Jesus come to show us by His life that God is love; He came to show us by His death that love gives to the uttermost. But 'showing us', in itself, would not have been enough. We would still have gone on failing, in spite of the example He gave, because of the disease of self-seeking in the heart of us, a disease which God calls sin. But 'by His stripes we are healed'—and it is then that His love can be shed abroad in our hearts.

A word which has been substituted for love in recent years is the word 'caring', because caring suggests love in action. Many will be familiar with the novels of E. M. Forster, and will be aware that the underlying theme of the best of them is that the central radiance of life is love. This—striking thought though it is, with its analogy drawn from the sun, which is our life force, the source of energy upon which our universe depends—is an essentially humanistic view, for it suggests that human love is enough, that it is sufficient of itself. We have only to look at the love of God as displayed in His Son, to see the insufficiency of even the best in human love.

Paul praying for the Christians at Ephesus, wished for them that they might know the love of Christ 'which passeth knowledge'. 'That Christ may dwell in your hearts by faith; that ye, being rooted and grounded in love, may be able to comprehend with all saints what is the breadth and length, and depth and height, and to know the love of Christ, which passeth knowledge . . .'

How can we know something which passes knowledge? It is like asking us to look at the whole sweep of the sky at once, or to plumb the depths of the sea with the naked eye, or to describe what lies behind the far horizon. No wonder Paul goes on to speak of the One who is able to do 'exceeding abundantly above all that we ask or think, *according to the power that worketh* in us'—for if he had not added this, we might well give up.

A recent visitor to the Holy Land took the trouble to measure the actual length that Jesus walked on His betrayal night. It was found that the distance He covered from the garden of Gethsemane to the judgment hall, from there to Pilate's palace, then back to Caiaphas, and from thence through the city to Calvary, was about eleven miles in all.

'All the way to Calvary He went for me'—this surely (not merely in physical measurements, of course), is the '*length*' to which love took Him for us. As has been already noted, He could have shown us, simply by example (so one might reason) what the love of God was really like; but this would not have been a full expression of this unfathomable quality. For ultimately, love must *redeem* the unlovable. Many of us miss out completely on this aspect of love—because we ourselves refuse to go *to the lengths* of admitting our unlovableness.

Dr. D. R. Davies, in his book *In Search of Myself* tells how he eventually discovered this hitherto unrecognized element in his own experience. As a Congregational minister in the thirties, he became a socialist and preached a 'social gospel'. People flocked to hear him, for he had the needs of the workers at heart. Outside his church, one could read this notice: 'This church stands instinctively for the social gospel, for the application of Christian principles in industry, politics and international affairs.' In his pulpit, the message of the Cross was glossed over. He believed that man's need was not salvation from sin, but improved social conditions. It might, perhaps, be said that his was a 'caring' ministry.

But there came a time when Davies began to feel the whole structure of his philosophy falling apart. He left the ministry and went to London, where he took up journalism. Here he became involved in all kinds of 'way-out' groups, and eventually finished up without a penny to his name, friendless, estranged from his wife, down and out in the fullest sense of the word.

He became a Marxist and went to Spain, where he came to realize, as never before, the bestiality of man. He returnd home to his wife, but although she had remained faithful to him through all his wanderings, he knew that his marriage was on the verge of ruin. One day, on a visit to the coast, he walked on the beach intent on ending it all. Grimly he waded into the deep sea. But as he plunged into the dark waters, something tremendous and staggering happened to him. Like a flash there came to him the blinding realization of what he was doing. He saw himself as he really was—full of sin and without hope.

'In the final anguish, hovering between life and death, I found myself, as I was, and in my utter nakedness and worthlessness I found God,' he writes. Later, he could say with complete certainty: 'No one can find God as Redeemer who still flirts with the possibility that one can redeem oneself. The final pride in one's own power must be broken. This is the rock of stumbling, the great offence of the cross to the mind of the fallen man, especially the fallen mind of modern man. To admit our powerlessness . . . this is to uproot man from his dearest delusion.'

The length of Christ's love took Him to Calvary. Yet love of ourselves, a deep-rooted, personal pride, holds us back so often from going to the length of admitting our need of His salvation.

When we think of the *breadth* of the love of Christ, we see His arms outstretched to those in need. Jesus had time for everyone. He was moved with compassion by the crowds who followed Him, because He saw them as sheep without a shepherd. He saw the blind, the deaf, the dumb; the lame, the mentally sick, the hungry; the grief-stricken, the sin laden, those possessed by evil spirits; the young, the middle aged, the old—and He stretched out His arms in healing love to them all. His love was all-embracing—He had no prejudices. He reached out His hand and touched the untouchable leper; he spoke words of compassionate forgiveness to the woman taken in adultery; He had room in His heart and time in His life for the social outcast; He swept aside not only racial prejudice but sex discrimination when He talked with the woman of Samaria. How shocked His disciples were to see Him talking not only to a foreigner—but a *woman* at that! This kind of outreaching love was strange to the religious leaders of the day. They were too busy making a good impression with their 'holy' law-keeping to have time for the basic needs of the common man.

Whenever I read the verses in Matthew 25 in which Christ exhorts His disciples to feed the hungry, visit the sick and the prisoner, to give shelter to the stranger and to clothe the naked, I am struck afresh by the gravity of sins of omission. 'Inasmuch as ye did it not to one of the least of these, ye did it not to me. *And these shall go away into everlasting punishment . . .*' It seems to me that one of the greatest dangers of our evangelical faith is to sit back and to say with comfortable assurance: 'I'm all right, Jack: I'm saved.'

F. B. Meyer said: 'The Cross stands for unselfishness, and those who claim to have been crucified with Christ must live not to themselves but to Him who died for them, and through Him for all that He cares and loves. The world is full of lonely, weary and desolate lives, to whom Christ would send us if we were ready for His use.'

Many professing Christians know little or nothing about the breadth of the love of Christ. They never reach out to their needy neighbour in love, lest the comfortable routine of their lives is disturbed. They are afraid to reach out and touch the untouchable, lest they find themselves out of their depth, involved in a way of life more broad and complex than they feel able to cope with. The same people will glibly say that the world needs love, that love is the answer. Yet they are not ready to meet the demands that this kind of love will make upon them. We are not prepared to ask God to direct us into the paths of the needy, because we are not prepared to pay the cost of such direction. We prefer to bury our heads in the sand of our own comfortable religiosity and murmur of love and caring.

And often, when we do venture out with our poor offers of love and care, when we do make an effort to be active in our loving, we discover, all too soon, how limited our resources really are. At the first rebuff, we shrink back into our shells like sensitive snails. At the first sign of discouragement we cry out peevishly that the task is beyond us, that we are not cut out for it, that it is a job for the experts. At the first sign of ingratitude, we limp away nursing our bruised pride and vow self-righteously that we will not again poke our noses in where we are not wanted. There is so much of self in our love. We expect, all the time, some kind of return, if it is only a feeling of gratification. How little we know of the selfless love of Christ! How little we comprehend the breadth of His love!

If there is one thing we shrink back from more than we shrink back from reaching out, it is from the prospect of being brought low. When we look at the *depths* to which Jesus went for us, we draw back in shame from such a love. 'Let this mind be in you,' says Paul to the Philippians, 'which was also in Christ Jesus, who, being in the form of God ... made Himself of no reputation, and took upon Him the form of a servant. ... He became obedient unto death, even the death of the cross ...'

It has been observed by some that even Paul would not have been called upon to die such a death as Jesus died, since crucifixion was reserved for the common man, for the criminal. He was King of kings, ruler of the universe, yet He suffered like a slave. He was God, yet He died the lowest of deaths—the death of a criminal. He was Creator of all things, and His home was Heaven, yet He descended into Hell for the sake of the created thing. Our minds cannot readily comprehend such humiliation; cannot begin to contemplate such depths of unfathomable love.

How much are we prepared to suffer for His name? The lives of the great Christians of our day fill us with shame and dismay. As we read incredible, nightmare experiences of those who have been tortured, imprisoned, beaten, separated for years from loved ones, we can hardly bear to follow the catalogue of their sufferings. That humankind should be able to survive such atrocities—that they should ever have emerged from such depths in their right minds—almost we question that we should be expected to read such accounts of human agony.

And when we hear of the tremendous sacrifices that so many make for the sake of Christ and His kingdom, of those who are ready to give up all that spells comfort and peace and happiness, and to live in appalling conditions, for the love of Christ, we are moved beyond words, shaken in our heart. The young couple who sold up their home—the home for which they had so carefully saved and planned—in order to go and work in some isolated corner of a foreign mission field; the Christians in Eastern Europe who live like paupers under the Communist régime because of the automatic loss of privilege and position accorded to those who name the name of Christ; women, like the wives of the Ecuador martyrs, who have sat at home with little children in their laps and watched their men go off to take the gospel message to a murderous and barbaric tribe—a single look into these kinds of depths makes us cling firmly to our foothold in 'normality'.

We cannot readily contemplate being brought low in any sense of the word. 'Humankind,' said T. S. Eliot, 'cannot bear very much reality.' For the truth is that there is very little 'reality' in the life which most of us call 'normal'. It is in the deeps and the heights of experience that reality is found. In the experience of grief, of personal loss, of suffering or of humiliation and renunciation we find our true selves. Yet how we shy away from these too. 'Lord spare me! Don't let me suffer! Others may be able to take it, but not me, Lord, not me!'

Yet when He takes us down into the depths with Him, we are amazed at the beauties we discover there, and we wonder why we should ever have shrunk from looking into the depths of His love.

In the Christian life there is an unfailing principle: the deeper we are prepared to go for love of Christ and for His Kingdom, the higher will be the pinnacles of joy we shall experience. The purest joy is born out of suffering, and only when we are crucified with Christ can we know the fullness of the life He gives.

> O, Love, that wilt not let me go . . .
> I dare not ask to fly from Thee!
> I lay in dust life's glory, dead,
> And from the ground, there blossoms, red
> Life that shall endless be!

In the Garden of Gethsemane, Jesus tasted the bitter dregs of the cup of suffering. But without the garden of suffering, there would have been no garden of resurrection. Without the depths there can be no heights. Because He humbled Himself and became obedient unto death, God has highly exalted Him, and given Him a name which is above every name! And we share with Him the heights of His love, when we are ready to share in His suffering.

In the lives of the saints, both past and present, this same note is struck—the heights of joy to which the sufferers rose—the heights of worship and praise and communion with the living Christ. Out of their despair, grows the lovely flower of victory. Visitors to churches in parts of the world where Christians are oppressed and persecuted tell of the tremendous spirit of devotion and jubilation to be felt in the worship of these people. Their faith is a vibrant, living thing, purified and refined on the altars of suffering.

So it is with those who are called upon to pass through the dark valley of sorrow and tribulation. When we emerge into the light, and climb the hillside which leads out of every valley, we experience heights of joy which we had never dreamed of before. I remember so well this sense of amazement which my husband and I felt just after the death of Frankie, and merely to read the words I wrote then evokes the preciousness of the experience.

We were (I wrote), 'somehow caught up to the very heavens on the mighty wings of God himself. From this, exalted height, we viewed, as it were, the rest of the world in a kind of dazzling isolation. We could not mourn, for there was no grief in our hearts. God had taken our sorrow and turned it, according to His promise, into joy.' Others who have passed through a similar valley have written to tell me that this, too, was exactly their own experience.

We cannot live for ever on the heights. We cannot bear that much reality. But it is in moments like these that we glimpse something of the height of the love of Christ.

Yes, what the world needs today—is love. But not the synthetic, two-dimensional substitute we offer so eagerly. It needs the four-dimensional love of Christ.

What greater prayer could Paul have offered for the church at Ephesus than that they should be rooted and grounded in this love, and that they might be able to comprehend with all saints what is the breadth and length and depth and height, and to know the love of Christ, which passeth knowledge?

Our loving heavenly Father,

We would thank You now for Your great gift of love to
    mankind.

We would thank You for all human love;

The love of parent for child; of child for parent;

The love of brother for sister; and the love between husband
    and wife;

For the touch of the hand and look in the eye which can
    speak love though no words be spoken;

For the love which has surrounded us since infancy, mould-
    ing our lives with gentle hands, and shielding us from
    the world's ills;

For love which serves, and does not count the cost; for love
    which has been faithful even unto death, and yet has
    not looked for any reward.

And yet, Lord, we know that even the most perfect of
    human love is but a faint reflection of that great love
    which is for ever burning in Your heart

For You are Love.

The very essence of Your being is Love.

It was love which made You send Your only begotten Son to
    be our Saviour, and love which made Him stretch out
    His hands to all in need. It was love which took Him to
    the cross, and love which cried: 'It is finished' when the
    final act of redemption was complete.

Lord, help us to understand something of the height and the
    depth and the length and the breadth of the Love of
    Christ, which passes knowledge,

That when others reach out toward us for a share of this
    love, we may not send them away empty.

Lord, we thank You that even in the darkest spot of earth
    some love is found;

That in the horror and the darkness of a world torn by sin
    and greed and suffering, love still shines out like faint
    stars, reflecting a little of Your light to those who have
    forgotten You, or never knew You.

Lord, we cannot contemplate a world without love;

And we who know You cannot contemplate a world with-
    out You.

Oh, hear us, we pray as we lift up our voices in prayer for all
    who are without You, and without hope in the
    world.

And hasten that day, we pray, when the earth shall be filled with the glory of God, as the waters cover the sea.
For the sake of the one who loved us, and gave Himself for us.

Amen

A Kind of Freedom

Voices
  Crying on the desert air:
    Crying of freedom, crying of despair.

'Free!
  God help us—we are free!
    Free to destroy, to abuse and to abase
      Ourselves and others . . .
        Free! God help us—we are free!'

For there is a kind of freedom
  Which traps the soul in a mesh;
  Which binds the human spirit
With elastic bands of flesh . . .

A Voice
  Crying in the wilderness:
    'If the Son shall make you free
      You shall be free indeed!'

But the voices,
  They go on crying.
    Out there in the desert, where we left them,
      They cry, and we pay no heed.

4

The Inner Liberty

It is always interesting to see the way in which modern art forms especially drama and the novel, reflect the current questionings and preoccupations of man. And although there is much, both in the realm of fiction and of drama, that we, as Christians, feel is outside of our boundary of what is wholesome and permissible, yet there are some writers whom we should not ignore.

Joyce Cary the novelist asks: 'Where are the Freudians of yesteryear? Where are the Marxists, the behaviourists? All of them have a little bit of truth wrapped up in a mass of nonsense. What you want to do is to dig out the truth, or as much of it as you can pry loose.'

This, I feel, is how the Christian must appoach the works of modern thinkers. Many of them have 'a little bit of truth wrapped up in a mass of nonsense'. They are bound to have, because, as human beings, we of necessity see 'through a glass darkly'. But the little bits of truth may be like precious jewels when they are dug out by non-Christian readers who, whether they know it or not, are condemned to live in a world without God. For this reason we may feel that we have something to learn from such writers as Graham Greene, William Golding, or Joyce Cary, though much that they write is unpalatable.

Graham Greene in his book *In Search of a Character* makes a comment which I find very interesting in the light of the fact that he is often described as a 'religious' novelist. I would not advise any Christian unused to modern literature to read Greene's novels in order to find out how true this description is—but all the same, this is what he has to say of himself and of his readers:

'I would claim, not to be a writer of Catholic novels but a writer who, in four or five books took characters with Catholic ideas for his material. None the less, for years—particularly after *The Heart of the Matter*—I found myself hunted by people who wanted spiritual help with spiritual problems that I was incapable of giving. Not a few of these were priests themselves . . .'

It saddened, yet challenged me, when I read this, to think that novels with as little spiritual truth in them as Graham Greene's have should move men to write to him for spiritual help—help which he says he could not give. Much of Graham Greene's fiction does show an awareness of the split in man's mind, the insidious pull of good and evil which results from the Fall: yet he provides no solutions. Graham Greene is, of course, a brilliant novelist, and it is not the task of the novelist to provide solutions to human problems, but only to present a picture of the human situation as he sees it.

Yet the people who do have the answers are rarely, if ever, brilliant writers. It seems sad that, given such a powerful medium as the novel in which to depict truth, there are so few writers who have themselves experienced the Truth as it is to be found in Jesus Christ. Or if they have, then they do not have great enough artistic skill to present it in a form which will be accepted by the intelligent reader.

Why is this? Perhaps the reason lies, basically in the fact that the artist, whether he be painter, musician, poet or writer, must, in order to be really great, be prepared to sacrifice everything to his art. For the Christian, this can never really be. No man can serve two masters, and the believer must obey the dictates of his Lord, not his art. This means that in the artistic sense he is not free. Even if he never writes a single word which might offend or sully the human mind, and makes that his only criterion, his only limitation, this, in itself, is enough to impair his impact as a creative artist. As soon as he begins to 'control' his creative gift, he limits its power. As a work of art, his writing must suffer. I do not say that no true believer can write a good novel, but I seriously doubt if he can write a great one.

Which is a pity when one considers the impact of such a book as William Golding's Lord of the Flies, a book which is often set as a school text book. This story concerns a band of small boys washed up on a desert island. Golding depicts in a disturbing almost savage fashion, what happens to this cross-section of juvenile humanity when separated from all external influences and set down in beautiful and ideal surroundings. The inner natures and natural desires of the boys come to the fore with disastrous results. What begins as

54

simple competitiveness and quarrelsomeness develops into a nightmare situation. The boys revert to barbarism of a most sinister kind, and evil prevails. When rescued at the end of the story, the principal character weeps 'for the end of innocence, the darkness of man's heart . . .' 'I'm afraid of *us*,' says one of the boys earlier on in the story when asked to define just what it was that he feared most on the island.

Though Golding so clearly believes in the old fashioned concept of 'original sin', he, like Graham Greene, has no answers to give. The reason is, of course, that he has not found a solution: he can, therefore, only diagnose the disease. He knows no cure. In another of his novels, *Free Fall*, he depicts a man looking back over his whole life and trying to decide at which point he himself became responsible for his own failure.

'In that lamentable story of seduction,' says the narrator, 'I could not remember one moment when, being what I was, I could do other than I did . . . Oh, the continent of a man, the peninsulas, capes, deep bays, jungles and grasslands, the deserts, the lakes, the mountains and the high hills! How shall I be rid of the kingdom, how shall I give it away?'

We hear in this cry an echo of St Paul's own words:

'Oh, wretched man that I am! Who shall deliver me from the body of this death?'

But, unlike William Golding, St Paul has the answer to his own question:

'*I thank God, through Jesus Christ our Lord!*'

Certainly, as a modern literary critic has said, there are few people now, Christian or not, who would reject the doctrine of original sin. Yet when it becomes a personal issue, man rejects it as strongly as ever he did. How free is man? To what extent is he able to become 'master of his destiny'? And why, when he is ready to admit the basic depravity of humankind, is he so unready to admit his own need for regeneration?

Another literary critic, writing about the work of William Golding, says that he is a 'genuinely religious novelist with a vision based on the concept of original sin, of the horrifying thinness of civilization, of the fragile barriers that lie between man and regression into barbarism and chaos.' He goes on to say that there is a danger in accepting the evil displayed in the horrors of our century as being '*the* fundamental truth about man'. Perhaps he is right, for we must never lose sight of the fact that man was first made in the image of God and therefore the potentiality in man is tremendous. What the modern writers of fiction and drama cannot give us is hope. They leave us, at the end of their works, in the same darkness and despair as when they began. Their message is not only that of recognizing the basic disease of humankind, but also that of the hopelessness of looking for a cure.

Although there is certainly a danger in depicting man as irretrievably depraved, there is perhaps, an even greater danger in overlooking, or denying, that man is, to use David's words 'shapen in iniquity'. When the scholars and psychologists of the earlier part of our century ditched the Biblical teaching of 'original sin', they infected our civilization with a disease which today rages at fever pitch. For we are now reaping the results of such thinking amongst our young.

For years now it has been fashionable to give children as much attention and as much freedom as is practicably possible, in the fond belief that a child, left to develop himself and express himself according to the dictates of nature, will become a more mature, more fully developed, emotionally stable and fulfilled person than his forebears were. What has happened as a result? We have a society in which lawlessness, permissiveness, mental breakdown, and moral decadence are commonplace. For man, when he is free to choose good or evil will choose, for the most part evil. 'The imagination of man's heart is evil from his youth,' observes the Lord in the story of Noah. Given enough rope, man will destroy himself. True freedom will never be found therefore, in lack of restraint. Rather the opposite. Thomas Farber, writing in *Tales for the Son of My Unborn Child*, says this:

'The freedom from work, from restraint, from accountability, wondrous in its inception, became banal and counterfeit. Without rules, there was no way to say no, and worse, no way to say yes.'

The young people of our day, many of whom are turning back again to the authority of the Bible, have discovered for themselves the bitterness of 'freedom'. They are crying out to be guided, to be led back into the paths of order and direction which they scorned and abandoned a decade or so ago.

'Why don't you stop explaining it to me, reasoning with me, and just tell me not to do it,' cried one young girl to a patient parent who was carefully trying to avoid being authoritarian and dictatorial over a matter of morals.

'Please mummy,' begged another teenager who had been invited to a 'doubtful' party, 'tell me I can't go!'

A young man complained that life was like being in a high-powered car in the middle of a desert. He could go any way he pleased; yet not only were there no signposts, but he could not control the car. What we have failed to realize—or to believe—is that humankind is born with a bent toward evil, and that unless he is restrained by parental control, and later, by a measure of authority in school, then he is unready to become a man because he has never learned to make moral choices.

Jesus said that whosoever commits sin is the servant of sin, and He went on to say that the only way to freedom is through Himself, the Son of God. 'Ye shall know the truth, and the truth shall make you free.' Many young people today are discovering this for themselves. They have been in bondage to sin, bound hand and foot by every kind of fleshly lust. They have had their freedom. They have helped themselves to anything they wanted, with no thought of the cost either to themselves or to others. They have exercised their so-called 'right' to do as they please. They have followed the dictates of their own hearts, confident, as they have been taught since babyhood, that only good can come of such 'healthy' self-fulfilment. We the older generation have turned them loose as it were into a world which (as John puts it) 'lies in the wicked one'; we have sent them out without a guide book, having already taken down the signposts. 'Make up your own minds about these things,' we have said. 'We would not presume to advise you. You are responsible human beings. You are free to be what you please.'

No wonder the so-called Jesus Movement is capturing the attention of so many of the young. The wheel has turned full circle. What seems like 'old hat' to many of the older generation, an out-dated Christianity they rejected when they were young, is startling good news to the young. No wonder so many of them are flocking to follow a Christ whom they are being made to see for the first time as a figure of strong authority as well as boundless love; a Man who stood up and told the people in no uncertain terms what God had to say to them; a Teacher who was not afraid to say that black was black and white was white; who demanded of His followers nothing less than complete submission to His will and His word.

Young people are hungry for this kind of strong meat. They have been fed on milk all their lives; they have been destroyed by the softness and spinelessness of a system of so-called 'authority' which refuses to set absolute standards for its young. They are, in fact, ripe for the gospel—if only we, the older generation, are wide enough awake to see it.

What is the gospel? The gospel is the good news of Jesus Christ, and it is set out clearly for us in the New Testament. God has said that man, ruined by the Fall, is in bondage to sin from the moment of birth. The only way in which mankind could be set free from such slavery, was for God to send His own Son to earth to show, by His life and His teaching, that God is Love; but that His love is holy as well as compassionate, and must therefore punish sin. But so great was the love of God, that He sent His only begotten Son to bear our sin, and the punishment for our sin on the cross. When we accept this by faith then the act of redemption takes place in our hearts, and we are free. Free from the judgment of God, free from the penalty of sin, free from the power of sin in our lives. This does not mean, of course that we do not sin again. But we become, from the time of our salvation, free from its bondage.

'Stand fast, therefore,' said Paul, 'in the liberty wherewith Christ hath made us free, and be not entangled again with the yoke of bondage.'

Paul himself knew all about the warfare between right and wrong that every Christian experiences. 'When I would do good, evil is present with me,' he says. But he can conclude by saying that it is Jesus Christ who gives us the victory—because we are now no longer under the control of our baser natures, but under the control of Christ Himself.

'*My chains fell off*', sang Charles Wesley, '*my heart was free! I rose, went forth, and followed thee!*'

And young people who have been to the cross of Jesus Christ for salvation, take up the strain and sing with joy that they are free—truly free for the first time in their lives.

We, the older generation had better start putting back the signposts as fast as we can. For, ultimately, the only kind of

58

freedom which has any meaning, and is of any value to the civilization of which we are a part, and of which our children are the future, is that inner liberty, the freedom of the inner man, that only Christ can give.

O, Jesus Christ, our Lord,
Who came to set men free,
To comfort the broken hearted, and to set at liberty the
   bruised,
Hear us now as we cry to You from the dungeons of our
   own hearts' needs;
Break, Lord, into the strongholds which we have bolted and
   barred against You;
Invade us with Your love, we implore You, and set us free.
O, Lord we have become slaves and servants to our own
   desires;
We have become self-centred, self-indulgent, self-orient-
   ated;
And therefore we have bound ourselves with chains, and we
   have no strength left in us, nor any health.
But hear us now, as we cry to You:
You who were bound and beaten, mocked and condemned
   to die the death of a criminal,
That we, Barabbas, might go free.
That we, the sinners, might be absolved from guilt;
You who died in agony that we might be redeemed;
Who rose again from the dead that we might share with
   You in Your victory, might be partakers of Your glori-
   ous liberty—
Hear us, we pray, and have mercy upon us.
For Lord, not only have we bolted and barred our own
   hearts against You, but we have made fetters for our
   children,
And have sent them, bound hand and foot into a world full
   of darkness and raging storm;
We have removed the old landmarks;
We have forsaken You, the fountain of living waters
And hewed out for ourselves cisterns,
Broken cisterns that will hold no water.
For ourselves and for our children,
We crave mercy, O, Lord,
And we crave it only by the merits of Your Cross,
O Jesus Christ our Lord,
Saviour of the world,

                                                        Amen

Invasion

Love came into my garden
  And, falling on her knees,
She kissed the barren, knotted roots
  Of the cold, dead trees.
    And straightaway, on every branch
    A golden flame was lit.

Joy came into my garden,
  Bird-bright and soaring high.
She touched the topmost branches
  With her wings' soft sigh.
    And straightaway the air was filled
    With shimmering, silver song.

Peace came into my garden,
  A clear deep-flowing brook.
And winding through the warmth and song
  Her way she took.
    And now my winter garden is
    A summer of delight.

5

The Inner Radiance

'What do you really want out of life?'

A young man replies with a sidelong smile:

'Money—success—'

'Just to be happy,' says a starry-eyed schoolgirl.

Both answers are really the same. The girl is just being more direct about it. For some reason, there is an element of 'unmanliness' in admitting to wanting to be happy. But in the last analysis, happiness is the ultimate goal of most of us.

It is, perhaps, typical of a fallen race that it should look outside itself for something which can only come from within. Malcolm Muggeridge once said in a broadcast talk that there is something quite ridiculous, and even indecent, in an individual claiming to be happy.

'Still more,' he continued, 'a people or a nation making such a claim. The pursuit of happiness, included along with life and liberty in the American Declaration of Independence as an inalienable right, is without question, the most fatuous which could possibly be undertaken. The lamentable phrase—the pursuit of happiness—is responsible for a good part of the ills and miseries of the modern world ... The pursuit of happiness, in any case, soon resolves itself into a pursuit of pleasure—something quite different—a mirage of happiness, a false vision of shade and refreshment seen across parched sand.'

We live in a hedonistic age. In the western world, at least, pleasure, in one form or another, appears to be man's chief aim in life. And because to modern man, pleasure and fulfilment are synonymous with material success, all his energies are bent toward this end. Aided by technology and education, he plunges headlong toward self-destruction, for he has never understood or heeded the words of Jesus when He said that it is the man who is prepared to lose his life who finds it.

'For what shall it profit a man if he gain the whole world and lose himself?'

At the end of the broadcast talk mentioned above, Malcolm Muggeridge made reference to Pastor Bonhoeffer, who was executed by the Nazis for his faith. As he faced death, Bonhoeffer's whole countenance shone with a radiance which confounded his executioners.

'In that place of darkest evil,' said Malcolm Muggeridge, 'he was the happiest man—he, the executed. I find this an image of supreme happiness.'

With all due respect to Mr Muggeridge, I would prefer to describe the radiance that shone from the martyr's face as 'joy'. Happiness is such a transitory thing. It comes and goes according to the force of the moment. 'Happiness happens,' says the children's chorus, 'but joy abides—in the heart that is stayed on Jesus.'

These simple words express a profound truth. Joy is an irrepressible effluence which has its source in the indwelling Christ. Joy is alive; joy is creative; joy is infectious. It is a light which cannot be put out by sorrow, by adversity, or by persecution. Joy is a miracle, because it is a fruit of the Spirit of God Himself.

There is an element of paradox in all truth, and we soon come to see that there is no joy without sorrow. These opposites are really two sides of the same coin. No man can know the joy which Christ offers until he has tasted sorrow for his own sinfulness and failure. In the book of Nehemiah there is a moving picture of the gathering together of men and women that they might hear the long neglected law of the Lord read aloud. As they listened, so the people began to weep. One by one they bowed down under the weight of their own failure, as exposed by the searching light of the Word of God. When Nehemiah saw the people weeping, he said a very wonderful thing.

'This day is holy unto the Lord your God' he cried. 'Mourn not, nor weep: *for the joy of the Lord is your strength* . . .' There follows a moving picture of the rejoicing of the people; a rich, deep rejoicing born out of sorrow for sin.

This is the 'joy of salvation' from which the tree of joy must grow. 'With joy,' writes the Psalmist, 'shall ye draw water out of the wells of salvation.' It was for this cause that Jesus, the Son of God, endured the Cross, despising the shame—'for the joy that was set before him'. Joy was one of the most precious of the trophies which Jesus brought back with Him from the grave. To those who have wept for the sins which nailed Him to the cross—to those who have mourned for the darkness of their own hearts, He gives the radiant light of His joy. *The joy of the Lord is your Strength.*

It comes as something of a surprise to find that Paul talks so much about joy in his epistles. One pictures him, perhaps, as a rather dour little man, a great theologian, but rather weighed down with the burden of his own vision—as theologians often are. But Paul is constantly exhorting the early Christians to rejoice. 'Rejoice in the Lord always—and again I say, rejoice!'

Paul speaks of 'longsuffering with joyfulness'—and he should know. In beatings, imprisonments, shipwreck and illness, he could say that he 'rejoiced in the Lord'. He exhorts us to rejoice not only when there is something to rejoice about, but all the time. 'As sorrowful,' he says, 'yet always rejoicing.'

C. S. Lewis wrote a book about his own spiritual journey from atheism to Christianity and called it *Surprised by Joy*. This, perhaps, is the most remarkable thing about joy—that it nearly always takes us by surprise. A Christian prisoner in one of Hitler's concentration camps wrote this:

'Not once have I been assailed by any doubt that what God wills even in this situation is just good. Not for one moment have I contended with Him. Therefore, despite some very gloomy hours, despair has remained far from me. Strange as it may sound, I have learned one thing in this prison—*to be joyful.*'

When I sat down to write the story of my daughter's death shortly after the ordeal was over, I described the days immediately preceding the end in these words: 'I remember waking up each morning, after a restless night, and feeling joy literally flooding my heart. Beside me, the laboured breathing of my little one told me that she was still with us. And I lifted up my heart to God in praise for yet another day in which to love and serve her . . .'

When I came to prepare the final draft of the manuscript for publication, I altered the word 'joy' to 'peace', because I was afraid that readers who had never passed through such an experience should misunderstand and be shocked that any mother was capable of feeling joy in her heart at such a time as this. In retrospect, I am surprised myself. The experience seems unreal, out of this world—as of course it was. But reading through the words I wrote at that time, I am able to taste again, in a measure, that 'miracle of joy'.

The fruits of the Spirit always take us by surprise, simply because they are not of our own making. Like the 'peace that passes understanding', the joy that sits side by side with sorrow and grief in the human heart is God-given. It has lit the faces of the martyrs down the ages, rung out like bells in the voices of those who have faced violent death and torture for naming His name, and shone like a light in the darkest corners of the earth. How the voice of Paul must have vibrated with it as he dictated his letter for the Romans to Tertius:

'For I am persuaded, that neither death, nor life, nor angels, nor principalities, nor powers, nor things present, nor things to come, nor height, nor depth, nor any other creature, shall be able to separate us from the love of God, which is in Christ Jesus our Lord.'

Sabina Wurmbrand, in her book *The Pastor's Wife*, tells of the seven nightmare years she spent in Communist prisons and labour camps. The unimaginable sufferings of those years make the average western mind shrink from even having to contemplate them. Interrogations, beatings, starvations and slave labour sent some women mad, while others succumbed to merciful death. Sabina was a shining witness to Christ in the dungeons and rat infested shacks where women lived like animals. In moments of special terror, other women clung to her like children to a mother, feeling a pathetic sense of safety in being able to touch someone in whom the spirit of God so obviously dwelt.

Not knowing whether her husband—who was a prisoner elsewhere, and for whose sake she herself was being held—was alive or dead; not having seen her young son since he was nine years old, this woman could nevertheless speak faithfully of Christ and of her trust in Him. When, eventually, she was released, her son—now a tall, teen-age lad—asked her:

'How could you bear all this without giving way and denying Christ?'

Sabina answered by telling him of a peculiarity in the Hebrew language where some future events are described in the perfect tense. The fifty-third chapter of Isaiah, for example, foretells the sufferings of the Messiah, but speaks of these events as belonging to the past, not the future. When Jesus was already on the path of suffering, He would have read of these events *as if they had already happened* Sabina explained:

'Joy is the *everlasting present* of the Christian spirit. I was in a heavenly place from which no one could move me. Where was the affliction through which I passed? To that most inviolable part of my mind, it belonged to the past. I lived the suffering long ago, while the present reality was delight in the closeness of the Lord.' Such thoughts are only to be found, fathoms deep, on the ocean bed of Christian experience. Paul would have understood:

'For our light affliction,' he said, 'which is but *for a moment* worketh for us a far more exceeding and eternal weight of glory, while we look, not at the things which are seen, but at the things which are not seen.'

'Rejoice,' said Jesus Himself, speaking of those who are persecuted for righteousness sake. 'Rejoice, and be exceeding glad: for great is your reward in heaven . . .'

'Count it all joy,' says James, 'when you fall into divers temptations (or various trials).'

'Weeping may endure for a night, but joy cometh in the morning,' sang David.

Sorrow and joy go hand in hand.

Not only is the Christian promised joy, but he is promised an overbrimming supply of it. When Jesus said that He had come that we might have life, He added: 'and that ye might have it more abundantly.' Similarly, not only did He wish us to have joy, but that our joy 'might be full'. The first three fruits of the spirit mentioned in Paul's list are love, joy and peace, and we soon come to realize how interdependent they are. Love is the flame He lights in our heart when we surrender our lives to Him; joy is the glow that flame gives off—a glow which we cannot hide; and peace is the warmth and light which floods our hearts when love and joy are there. But it is all too easy to allow the lamp of our joy to grow dim because the quality of our love has grown poor. The secret of a rich and full joy is to 'abide' in the love of Christ.

Jesus said: 'If ye keep my commandments, ye shall abide in my love; even as I have kept my Father's commandments, and abide in His love. These things have I spoken unto you that my joy might remain in you, and that *your joy might be full.*'

What did He mean? He meant that the measure of our joy is obedience to Him. Only inasmuch as we are dependent upon Him for our ability to love, to serve, to suffer, to rejoice, and to know victory in our personal lives shall we experience the fullness of joy that He speaks of. For He is the source of our very life, and the moment we forget this and become self-sufficient, we become unfruitful branches of the vine.

'As the branch cannot bear fruit of itself except it abide in the vine; no more can ye, except ye abide in me.'

The branch has no life of its own. Some of us need to be constantly reminded of our own inadequacy. This is a painful process, and we always shrink from pain. But the tree which has been pruned regularly by a loving and faithful gardener, is the tree which bears the most fruit. One of the hardest lessons to learn is that our own love will not generate any true joy because it is too poor a thing. There is so much of self in our own.

But the love of Christ is perfect in every respect, a love which passes knowledge, a divine love. Only inasmuch as we are able to reflect something of His perfect love to the world around us shall we be of any use to Him. The moment we begin to lose sight of His perfection and begin to take pleasure in our own goodness, our own feelings for others, our own natural sympathy for our fellow beings, then we take upon ourselves a 'glow' which has nothing to do with true joy.

'Herein is my Father glorified,' said Jesus, 'that ye bear much fruit.'

Are we really concerned with bringing glory to God? Do we see this as the sole purpose of our salvation? 'So shall ye be my disciples.'

It is to His disciples alone that He gives the final promise:

'These things have I spoken unto you, that *My joy* might remain in you, and that *your joy might be full.*'

Dear Lord Jesus Christ,
Source of all joy,
Whose very Person glowed and radiated with the joy that
    comes of being linked with the Father,
Give us, we pray, this precious gift of joy.
Kindle the spark of love in our hearts
Until it burns and glows—a living flame—filling our lives
    with warmth and radiance,
And shining out of us
Into the darkness of the world around.
Many waters cannot quench love,
For love is strong as death.
And nothing can put out the flame that You have lit in our
    hearts.
But so often we ourselves let the fire burn low,
By our own failure and unbelief,
By our own desire for glory,
By our own greed for personal gratification.
And so often we forget that the source of our love,
The root of our joy,
Is Yourself alone.
So help us to abide,
So help us to rely entirely upon Yourself,
That no matter what life may bring, and no matter how men
    may try to quench our fires,
We may burn on, love on, shine on,
And that others may be drawn toward the radiance,
Knowing it comes from an inner source,
From the source of all joy,
Which is Jesus Christ our Lord.
We ask it for the sake of His glory alone.

                                                    Amen

Gifts

Lord, give me a blessing,
  You know I need a blessing . . .
But be careful not to touch
  Any of my precious things—
Won't you, Lord?
  I really want a blessing,
Only—well, it won't be painful,
  Will it, Lord?
You know how very sensitive I am—
  So be careful, when You bring my blessing,
Not to tread on anything—
  Won't you, Lord?

Lord, give me this mountain,
  I've always wanted a mountain,
As you know, Lord.
  Yes, I really want this mountain—
Only will you go up there first, Lord,
  And smooth it out for me?
Some of those rocks look rather sharp—
  Could You clear them out of my path
And maybe level some of it off a bit—
  If You don't mind Lord?
Only, You know I never was much of a climber,
  But I've always wanted a mountain—
As You know, Lord.

Lord, give me your likeness,
  Only, please go very carefully
With the one I've got.
  I'm quite attached to it, really;
After all, I've had it a long time now . . .
  But You know what I really want
Is to be like You—
  So, give me Your likeness, Lord—
If it isn't too much trouble
  For either of us, Lord.

I heard Him sigh, I think,
And shake His head a little.
  'And what good is a blessing
Or a mountain,
Or a likeness
If I simply bring them to you on a plate?
  No, my child, I've news for you,
For if you really want them,
  Then you'll need to come and fetch them,
And that is quite some journey—
  So how about it? Are you ready?
Because I am—when you are.'

6
The Inner Cry

From the many letters I have received from readers of *Beyond the Shadows*, and from the numerous conversations I have subsequently had with people of every kind, I find that it is not so much the problem of their own suffering which baffles most people, as the problem of the suffering of the innocent. On the whole, people do not ask, overmuch, 'Why should I suffer?' What they do ask is, 'Why should my child (or my wife, or my father, or the helpless, starving millions in Asia) suffer, when they have done nothing to deserve it?'

Some time after Frances died, I received a letter from another mother whose child of five had died of the same disease. I replied to her letter, seeking to pass on to her something of the wonder of the experience through which we had passed. This was her reply:

'It was very good of you to write to me, and I have read and re-read your letter a number of times. We were so deeply sorry about Frances, and although you have such tremendous faith, I am sure you have your moments when your heart is breaking for her. At those times, you can think of me, and be sure that I most deeply understand and feel for you.

'I have been intending to write you a few lines for weeks, but your letter is so full of a completely sure belief in God that I cannot think what to say. You have found real comfort in your faith.

'What has prompted me to write is a report in today's newspaper of a father who killed his son Richard, aged twelve years, because the son was crying in pain from cancer of the spine, and the father could stand it no longer. This has upset me terribly.

'Our little boy, who was five when he died, suffered so much pain in his feet and legs every few weeks, for the twelve months of his illness. He could not stand the bed clothes touching him, and there was nothing we could do for his pain. Sometimes, when this was bad, I have been up in the night and nearly hysterical with anguish. This I don't bother to tell others, but I can tell it to you. After two and a half years, the loss of our little boy still hurts badly. I find that to go on living and smiling through each day and week I just have to shut my mind to his suffering, which sounds so heartless.

'So you see, although both my husband and myself have always thought we were Christians, we are completely unable to reconcile a child's suffering and a loving Father in Heaven. No loving Father could allow it if He was at all capable of stopping it. On the other hand, we have gained our only comfort from the Church, and our vicar here was wonderful to us. Also, we are afraid not to believe in God, in case we never see our little boy again. So I should say we are "rebel Christians" . . .'

When I read this letter, my heart ached for the unknown writer, whom I had never met. What agony, what torture she was passing through still—even two years after her tragedy! As I read of the anguish she had suffered in the face of her child's suffering, I relived our own anguish in similar circumstances. But the terrible thing to me about this other parent's suffering was that, in their innermost being, she and her husband were bearing it *alone*. The vicar, she had said, had been a tremendous help . . . But what of Christ? Did they know Him? 'We are rebel Christians,' she had said. . . . But there is no such thing as a 'rebel' Christian. The very idea is a contradiction in terms, for the essence of Christianity lies in submission and surrender.

As I went about my daily tasks, the burden of this suffering woman, and millions like her, weighed heavily upon my heart. I could not forget her, nor the tortured father who had killed his suffering son.

To many reading the brief newspaper report, such a story must have been a window on a nightmare world. Not a soul anywhere would condemn that father's action. One small detail caught my attention as I read it: the mother of the dying boy was in church at the time . . . I tried to imagine her homecoming—the gas-filled room, the twisted body of the young lad, at peace at last; the grief torn, broken husband . . .

Then I pictured the writer of the letter I had just received, reading of the incident, and her mind turning instinctively toward me and the letter I had written her. What would I have to say about this, she wondered? What indeed! I sat with the blank page before me wondering how I would dare to employ mere words as an answer to such an anguished cry for help. Finally I wrote this:

'My heart went out to you when I read your letter. How can I begin to answer it? I cannot bear to think that after two and a half years you are still suffering such agony of mind. You say that you just have to shut your mind to your little boy's sufferings—but his sufferings are over for ever! I am quite sure that he wouldn't want you to go on grieving for him in this way. Terrible though his illness was, I am certain that your mental suffering now is far more than his physical sufferings were. Just think for a minute—if his pains had been the result of some awful accident, and if, after a long period he had finally got better, he would by now have completely forgotten how badly he had suffered. Children are like that. They don't suffer mentally, as we do when we are in pain. Our sufferings are made up of all sorts of things, apart from the actual pain—dread of the next pain, rebellion and questioning over the whole business, anxiety for the future—all go to make the sufferings of an adult so hard to bear.

'To watch a child suffer is one of the most agonizing things possible. There were times with Frances when I cried out: "Oh, God, why couldn't it have been me?" We feel that we would far rather bear the pain ourselves than see our own child suffer.

'What you cannot accept is the thought that God does not step in and stop the innocent child's suffering. Faced with the terrible example of the little boy you mention, who had cancer of the spine, there seems just no satisfactory answer to this dark mystery. "If God is in control," one may say, "surely He can stop the innocent from suffering?" I do not pretend to have any complete answer to this.

'But this I do know—that when Jesus Christ stood looking over the city of Jerusalem, knowing, as He did, what awful sufferings were to befall its people throughout the ages, His heart was broken as He cried out: "Oh, Jerusalem, Jerusalem, thou that killest the prophets and stonest them which are sent thee, how often would I have gathered thy children together as a hen gathereth her chickens under her wings—*and ye would not!*"

'When Jesus conquered sin on the cross, He did not do

away with it. He made a way of escape for the individual who confesses his need, freed him from the consequences, and gave power to overcome it in our own lives. Suffering is one of the by-products of evil, and in the natural order of things, we can none of us escape it. But the Christian shares in the victory of the cross—a comprehensive victory which includes not only sin, but all its by-products. It therefore follows that sickness, sorrow and grief can have no *ultimate* power over the believer.'

But the innocent—what about the *innocent*? It seems obvious that in order to prevent the suffering of the innocent, it would be necessary for God to be constantly contravening the laws of nature. And although we may retort: 'Well, why doesn't He? He's all powerful, isn't He?'—we must realize that a world in which the innocent were never allowed to suffer is beyond our imagining. It would be quite another world order from the one in which we find ourselves. If, for example, each time a car load of people were involved in an accident, all young children were somehow miraculously spared, other questions would soon be raised: 'Why were the children spared and their parents taken?' might be the cry. 'How cruel, how unjust of God!' For it is the natural tendency of man to blame God for what cannot be changed, and it seems virtually impossible to give any satisfactory answer to the man or woman who does not know God *personally* as a God of love.

Even when we do know Him as Saviour, it is not easy to accept the fact of suffering in our lives—and least of all in the lives of those we love. If we could see suffering in relation to eternity, we might find a measure of comfort.

'Our light affliction,' said Paul, 'which is but for a moment, worketh for us a far more exceeding and eternal weight of glory . . .' Suffering, if we could but see it, is relative. So is the ultimate tragedy—death. The death of a child strikes horror in any heart, but there is a sense in which every mother 'loses' her children. If Frankie had not died at the age of ten, she would, at the time of writing this, be seventeen years old. She might, I suppose bear little resemblance to the lively affectionate little girl whose memory I hold so dear. In one sense I should have 'lost' that ten-year-old, even though my daughter still lived.

I have talked with many mothers since the publication of my story—some of them mothers of sick or handicapped children, some of them bereaved mothers, a few the mothers of wayward, difficult teen-agers. Of all the women who have bared their hearts to me, those in the last category have seemed to me to be in the greatest need of compassion. So deep has been the suffering of some that they have confessed to feeling they would rather their children had died young as Frankie did, than that they should have become the terrifying strangers that they now are. Death, it must be seen, is by no means the worst fate that can befall a child. Jesus Himself warned that the greatest menace we mortals can face is not the enemy which destroys the body, but the insidious, corrupting forces which destroy the soul. The thought of a dead child being 'safe in the arms of Jesus' may have an element of Victorian sentimentality in it, but for me it expresses, none the less, a precious truth. As far as Frankie is concerned I stake all on the words of Jesus when He said that none should ever pluck His children from His hand.

In the deep compassion that we have for the suffering of others—especially for suffering of the innocent, there is a danger that we might overlook the fact that suffering *in our own lives* can be of great value. Robert Louis Stevenson, who knew a great deal about suffering from his own experience said:

'That which we suffer ourselves has no longer the same air of monstrous injustice and wanton cruelty that suffering wears when we see it in the case of others.'

Anyone who has passed through a time of suffering, and has come through it the richer for the experience, will confirm this observation. A woman who had known much physical pain said this: 'Through my own experiences I have learned that it is only in the state of perfect suffering that the Holy Spirit works many marvellous things in our souls. It is when our whole being lies perfectly still under the hand of God, when every faculty of the mind and will and heart are at last subdued; when we stop asking God questions and crying "Why, Lord, why?" when we seek only the Lord and His will, then He will come to us and say—"It is enough".'

Where is faith without trial to test it;
Or patience, with nothing to bear;
Or experience, without tribulation to develop it?

We forget that when we suffer, we learn lessons we could

learn in no other way. It is only through submission and obedience that we can become the kind of people God wills us to be. In any kind of suffering, the individual concerned finds himself in a state of complete helplessness. There is nothing he can do to relieve his sufferings. He is cast entirely upon God. If he kicks out in rebellion against what has befallen him, then he only inflicts greater suffering upon himself. But if he submits, and makes himself yielding and pliable in the hands of the Potter, he will find that God is making something beautiful for Himself.

> *Ah! must—*
> *Designer infinite!—*
> *Ah! must Thou char the wood ere Thou canst limn with it?*

The answer, unwelcome though it may be, is yes. Paul affirms time and time again that no suffering is welcome at the time, but its end results are always worthwhile. Providing, of course, that we accept the suffering with humility and trust.

Throughout the teachings of Jesus Christ in the gospels we can trace a series of spiritual paradoxes. Jesus taught that it is the meek who inherit the earth, that it is the mourners who know what joy is, that it is the man who humbles himself who will be the greatest, and that it is the man who loses his life who will find it. When Jesus hung upon the cross. He was displaying another great paradox: it is the victim who is the victor, and there is no crown without a cross. T. S. Eliot put it this way:

> *In order to arrive there*
> *To arrive where you are, to get from where you are not,*
> *You must go by a way wherein there is no ecstasy.*
> *In order to arrive at what you do not know*
> *You must go by a way which is the way of ignorance.*
> *In order to possess what you do not possess*
> *You must go by way of dispossession . . .*

How we strive and struggle against the way of dispossession, the way of suffering, the way of the cross! Even Jesus Himself, in the garden with the weight of our humanity heavy upon His shoulders prayed that the bitter cup might pass from Him—'if it be possible' ... But it was not possible. For it was through His suffering that the created world must be redeemed.

When we suffer as Christians, we are sharing in the sufferings of our Saviour. Paul rejoiced that he was considered worthy to suffer with Christ. He regarded suffering always in this light, adding that he reckoned the sufferings of this present time are not worthy to be compared with the glory that God shall reveal in us.

All suffering has the appearance of defeat, as does every kind of passivity. But Jesus, the suffering servant, became the very personification of submission and passivity in order to show that the fruit of surrender is victory, that he that loses his life shall find it.

'And one of the elders answered, saying unto me, "What are these which are arrayed in white robes? And whence came they?" And I said unto him, "Sir, thou knowest." And he said unto me, "These are they which came out of great tribulation, and have washed their robes and made them white in the blood of the Lamb. Therefore they are before the throne of God, and serve him day and night in his temple: and he that sitteth on the throne shall dwell among them. They shall hunger no more, neither shall they thirst any more, neither shall the sun light on them, nor any heat. For the Lamb which is in the midst of the throne shall feed them, and shall lead them into living fountains of waters: and God shall wipe away all tears from their eyes." '

This is His answer to the inner cry from the suffering heart.

O, blessed Lord Jesus,
Who suffered on the cross for me,
Bearing in Your body not only my sins, but the dark horror
*   of the whole world's evil,*
And with it, all the griefs and the sorrows and the sicknesses
*   of humankind,*
Open now, to me Your great heart of compassion,
Incline Your ear to hear my cry,
My bitter cry of anguish,
A cry too deep for words.
Lord, I have so many questions, there are so many things I
*   do not understand;*
But have mercy on me, I pray, O Lord,
And touch the chill gloom of my mind's darkness
With the warmth and light of Your love.
You are Love.
Enfold me with Yourself, then, merciful Lord,
That I may be deeply conscious of this one thing:
That You are Love; that You love me; and that in Your Love
*   I am safe for ever.*
Then, Lord, take all my questions,
I surrender them to Your care;
Take all my rebellion,
I surrender it to Your control.
Take me, O great Potter, poor clay that I am,
I surrender myself into Your unfailing Hands,
Content to know that You are making
Something beautiful for Yourself
And for Eternity.
So be it, Lord;
I bow, now, to Your inscrutable, yet infallible wisdom,
Your boundless, unshakeable love.
And I rest in quiet assurance,

For Your Name's sake,
Amen

High Tide

'Rest in the Lord,
     wait patiently for Him . . .
Let not your heart be troubled
     neither let it be afraid . . .'
So came the rhythmic soothing
     of His whispers on my ear,
Like the lapping of cool waters
     on the burning rocks of fear.

But the sun still blazed
     while the waters were receding
And the rocks lay in mute agony
     Awaiting their return . . .
Oh, soon must end this noontide,
     surely, soon relief must come
From the scorching knowledge of His will
     and fear that must be dumb!

'Perfect love—' I heard You say it—
     'Perfect love casts out all fear'.
But Lord, You know my love is such
     a feeble, struggling thing . . .
Then came the tide, Thy love's strong tide,
     and now it covers me
With its cooling depth of perfect peace:
     for I am lost in Thee.

7

The Inner Rest

Ever since Cain raised his hand with murderous intent against his brother Abel, thus giving vent to his anger, his jealousy and his desire for supremacy, man has been striving against man in an insane quest for power. Blood-lust and violence are surely the two grossest evils which afflict our world, and almost since the beginning of time, wars have raged in some corner of the earth. All through history, right up to the present day, each sunrise has awakened some innocent soul to a day of grief, terror or total destruction.

Next to 'love', the theme which young people sing about more than anything else is that of peace. On the whole, modern youth is violently opposed to war in every form. And well they might be, when they have been born into a world torn and ravaged by every kind of strife, bloodshed and lawlessness. Jesus said, when speaking of the last days, that there would be 'upon the earth, distress of nations, with perplexity ... men's hearts failing them for fear, and for looking after those things which are coming on the earth ...' For modern man, whether he be old or young, there is no escape from these spectacles of war and horror, for we are confronted daily, in our newspapers, or on our television screens with scenes of carnage which many of our forebears would have quailed to contemplate. It may be argued, in fact, that we are in danger of becoming immune to the suffering of others. Yet deep in the hearts of many folk today I believe there is a sense of despair and fear for themselves and for their children.

Today, more than ever before, we need to take a fresh hold on the promise which Jesus Christ made to His disciples nearly two thousand years ago.

'Peace I leave with you', He said. 'My peace I give unto you. Not as the world giveth give I unto you. Let not your heart be troubled, neither let it be afraid'.

When considered in the light of events in any war-torn country, this statement of our Saviour's is staggering, to say the least. For He promised peace *in spite of* life's evil, in spite of life's pressures, in spite of life's sorrows, and in spite of life's uncertainty. This kind of comprehensive peace can only be known by the man or woman who is indwelt by the Holy Spirit of Christ Himself.

In recent years, the reality of evil must have presented itself to every thinking man in no uncertain way. No-one witnessing, or reading of, the horrors in Ireland, or Viet Nam, could possibly deny that there is evil in the human heart. Anyone who can throw a bomb which will kill and mutilate innocent shoppers and little children, or gun down impartial civilians in the streets, must be motivated by evil impulses of the grossest kind. Anthony Burgess, novelist and critic, in his book on the modern novel, said that to present day thinkers, the theory of original sin is no longer considered to be a laughing matter. 'We have all come to feel,' he says, 'a powerful and desperate guilt since the revelations of Belsen and the blasting of Hiroshima: there are few of us, now, who would reject the doctrine of original sin.'

When the Rev. Bickersteth wrote his well-known hymn on 'Peace' nearly a hundred years ago, he confronted us with this problem of evil in the very first verse. Each verse of this hymn is made up of a question and an answer, and each one presents us with some obstacle which might well rob the Christian of the peace Christ promised him.

'Peace, perfect peace—in this dark world of sin?' asks the hymnwriter. And back comes the answer: 'The blood of Jesus whispers peace *within*.'

Here we have the secret of real peace of mind and heart. For what worries us, basically, is not so much the evil and darkness in the world around us, but the seeds of it which we find hidden in our own hearts. The impulse which makes us put our own good before the good of another; the demon which makes us lash out, verbally or otherwise, at those who get in the way, or who wound our self-esteem; the appetites which fill our minds with thoughts and desires we would rather not own, and for which we make desperate, peevish excuses—these are the things which remind us of the darkness within. A one-time journalist responsible for the letter page on a national paper said that a large percentage of the letters received were from people haunted by feelings of guilt. Any Christian worker will find out before long that the basic need of the human heart is to find peace with God—to know, with certainty that somehow we will be able to stand, one day, in the presence of a holy God, uncondemned.

But it is one thing to accept that God sent His son to earth to die for the sins of the whole world, and another thing altogether to accept that He died for our own personal guilt and failure to meet God's standards. Only the Holy Spirit can convict a man of sin, for 'the god of this world has blinded the eyes of those who believe not'. But when, by faith, we respond to the Spirit's convicting power and confess our need of salvation, then the glorious peace of God flows into our hearts. 'Therefore', says Paul, 'being justified by faith, we have peace with God, through our Lord Jesus Christ'.

The preciousness of this kind of peace must be experienced to be believed. I could not live with myself, or face each coming day if it were not mine. And furthermore, it is the key to every kind of peace the heart can crave—as the Rev. Bickersteth must have known when he wrote his hymn.

'Peace, perfect peace—with thronging duties pressed?' he asks in the second verse. And then the answer: 'To do the will of Jesus—this is rest.'

We all know something about the pressures of life. It is one of the paradoxes of this machine age that we are surrounded on all sides by labour-saving devices, yet the pace at which we live is reaping a harvest of stomach ulcers, thromboses, and in many cases, complete nervous collapse. The number of people who cannot sleep at night without some kind of sedation is alarming. Those of us who are the parents of young people can find the psychological pressures of the society in which we live tremendous. Sometimes we may feel that no matter how well we may teach our children and train them toward a God-centred view of life, we are powerless against the subtle forces of evil arrayed against us. For we live in an age when the study of man, by man and for man has completely ousted all concepts of a divine and moral law outside of ourselves.

'Woe unto them,' Isaiah warned, 'that call evil good, and good evil; that put darkness for light, and light for darkness; that put bitter for sweet, and sweet for bitter!' Yet this is exactly what is happening today. Evil is actually being exalted under the guise of 'good'. The prophet concludes by warning that this happens when people forsake the truth of

God's unchanging law, and put their own wisdom in its place. The result is that our young people are subject to tremendous pressures from voices of so-called authority on every side.

It may sound like an over-simplification of life's problems to say, with the hymn writer, that peace comes when we 'do the will of Jesus', yet this, surely, is the only solution. No one can claim that they do not have access to God's guide-book. In this country, the Bible is available to all. As Christians, we must be so open to the leading of the Holy Spirit, so ready to obey His Word, so conscious of our dependence upon Him, that in every detail of our lives, and at every turn, we reach out like children, to Him.

An old lady I know—well into her eighties—told me, in an excited voice not long ago, that she had found a marvellous promise in the Bible which had really made her feel small! The promise was that God 'had *commanded* His peace' for her! How dare she doubt, she said, when God had *commanded* such a thing for her! We can surely all learn a lesson from this.

'Don't worry over anything whatever,' says Paul to the Philippians; 'tell God every detail of your needs in earnest and thankful prayer, and the peace of God which transcends human understanding, will keep constant guard over your hearts and minds as they rest in Christ Jesus.'

Peace, perfect peace—by thronging duties pressed?
To do the will of Jesus, that is rest.

We forget that our Heavenly Father is always ready to reveal His way to those who humbly seek it: and having done His will, we can leave the rest to Him.

Sometimes life deals us a blow which takes the very ground from under our feet. It is at times like this that we discover the meaning of real, deep peace. We may be sailing along quite placidly on the ocean of life, when suddenly, like the disciples on the lake, we run into an unexpected storm. It may take the form of bad news, a serious illness, the death of a loved one: sorrow, when she strikes, has a way of striking suddenly. How can we know peace when the very foundations of our lives are being shaken?

Peace? with sorrows surging round?
On Jesus' bosom, nought but peace is found.

Billy Graham used the following little word-picture to illustrate the peace God gives at times like these:

'The storm was raging. The sea was beating against the rocks in huge, dashing waves. The lightning was flashing, the thunder was roaring, the wind was blowing: but the little bird was sound asleep in the crevice of the rock, its head tucked serenely under its wing. That is peace: to be able to sleep in the storm!'

During the first critical weeks of our daughter's illness, with the news of the hopelessness of her condition still fresh in our minds like an open wound, it was a source of real wonder to my husband and myself that we were able to *sleep*. We expected to lie awake in an agonizing turmoil of mind, yet we were given this deep sense of peace, a peace which baffled us.

I did not think, I did not strive,
The deep peace burned my me alive.

So wrote the poet John Masefield. He was speaking for countless Christians who have found themselves burned into a new awareness of themselves and of their God by the fires of sorrow. 'Mystical?' asks Sarah Anne Jepson. 'No, a miracle! His peace is another one of His blessings which cannot be explained, but which is daily experienced by the believer walking in fellowship with Him.'

But it is not just the terror of the present which robs us of our peace, not just the agony of the moment which must be borne, though that is often bad enough. What about the future? What of tomorrow's world?

Peace, perfect peace—the future all unknown?

But listen to the answer:

Jesus we know, and He is on the throne!

We do not need to be in a war-torn country in order to fear the future. We are afraid of so many things. We are afraid for our children in this age of crumbling foundations, and we are afraid for the world situation of tomorrow; but we also fear old age, loneliness, financial insecurity, job redundancy and the threat of possible illness. The Christian has no guarantee against any of these things—yet fear should have no place in his heart.

'God is the perfect source of strength,' Sarah Anne Jepson reminds us. 'A continual dependence on Him keeps our spirits calm and serene, and yields a holy confidence which triumphs over the turbulence of living in these troubled times. Complete trust in Him is the best fortification against persecution, deprivation, unfair treatment, bitterness or pain. Nothing but the plan and peace of God provides this quietness and assurance. God can give this peace with His protection from evil, and can keep us with His gracious care.'

'The plan and peace of God . . .' We need to continually remind ourselves of God's sovereignty. Once we grasp the wonder of this, there is nothing left for us to fear! We are in His hands. I was deeply moved by the words of a young woman who had been passing through a period of great trial. Her husband was ill and out of work, and she was expecting her second child. The complexities of her situation were such that they cannot be recounted here, but suffice to say that she reached a point where she was at the end of her tether. Some time later, she told me that it was at this crucial time in her life that she read my book, and in doing so, found hope shining once more amid the darkness of her troubles.

'It was the sovereignty of God,' she told me; 'that is what came through to me from your story. The tremendous truth that He is in control, and that no matter how dark the future may seem, nothing and nobody can pluck us out of His hands.'

Jesus we know—and He is on the throne!

In his book *Ring of Truth*, the Rev. J. B. Phillips tells of the many truths he rediscovered for himself while translating the *Letters to Young Churches*. One of the verses which came to him with a new light was Paul's magnificent poem of assurance at the end of Romans chapter eight, when he says that he is persuaded that nothing can separate us from the love of God which is in Christ Jesus. 'For,' says Paul, in J. B. Phillips' rendering of the Greek, '*in the midst* of all these things we are more than conquerors, through Him that loved us.'

It was that phrase 'in the midst of' which so struck the mind of the translator. That Christians, even in the middle of all kinds of adversity, in the very throes of sorrow and anxiety and foreboding of the future should be overcomers! This is the wonder of it. For peace is that positive quality which fills the heart of the true believer and shuts out despair and defeat; peace is that incredible thing which wells up from within when all is darkness and gloom. It is not just a vacant space, an absence of fear and tension: it is a vivid consciousness of the very presence of the Prince of Peace Himself.

And nothing can shut out His presence—not even death, the final enemy. That is why the Rev. Bickersteth could not end his great hymn without encompassing this thought:

Peace, perfect peace—death shadowing us and ours?
Jesus has vanquished death, and all its powers!

The Christian can look death in the face, unafraid—can go out to meet him, as it were, with a song of triumph on his lips!

Lord Inman, one time chairman of the great Charing Cross Hospital tells a moving story about a young girl of seventeen who was dying of cancer. Lord Inman tells how he could hardly bear to pass through the ward where this girl lay, knowing the inevitability of what lay before her. Sometimes he saw her parents sitting by her bedside, and their calm, courageous countenance filled him with amazement and tore at his heart strings. Then one Sunday he happened to be in that particular ward at the time of the B.B.C. programme of hymn singing. The hymn which was being sung was 'Abide with me', and as the dying girl listened, so she began to join in and sing.

I fear no foe, she sang, with Thee at hand to bless.
Ills have no weight, and tears no bitterness.
Where is death's sting, where, grave thy victory?
I triumph still if Thou abide with me!

Lord Inman stood transfixed, for the poor, emaciated face of the young girl was radiant with a personal faith. Those words were her testimony! She meant every word she sang. She knew what lay before her, but she was not afraid. There

89

was a deep peace in her heart that all the powers of Satan could not reach.

When Jesus promised us His peace, it was this vast, all-encompassing peace He had in mind. He emphasized that He was not offering the kind of peace the world gives, but His own deep peace. The world offers us a tranquillizer to calm our nerves; a good film to help us forget our troubles; a romantic novel to trick us into thinking that life can be like that. Or it offers a stiff drink to dull our senses and our reason, a shot of heroin to make us high; or, more subtle still it offers the lure of material possession, the glitter of wealth to take our minds off our real needs. The peace the world offers is a hoax, a mirage, a cup of salt water to mouths parched with thirst.

But Jesus offers a peace the world cannot take away; a peace which will weather all the storms of life; a peace which springs up eternally in the heart where He himself reigns.

O, Prince of Peace, Saviour of mankind,
Who came to bring everlasting peace to the hearts of men,
Forgive me that I am so often fretful,
So often anxious, so often afraid.
Forgive me that I so often look to the world for comfort,
That I take refuge in escapes of one kind and another,
That I show so little faith in Your promises,
Or in Your love.
Lord, help me to open up the floodgates
Of my inner being
And let Your deep peace flow in.
Fill me, flood me, cover me, I pray;
So that when the wild gales come,
And the waves tower high,
I may still rest quietly
At the deep, inviolable source,
The central calm of Your peace.
Help me to shut out all the clamouring voices
Until I hear only Your voice of quiet command:
'Peace, be still;
Be still.
Be still and know
That I am God . . .
For ever and ever
World without end,'

Amen

Coming, Lads?

When you come to think about it, lads,
The Master did some very funny things.
Remember that day when He sent us to buy meat?
And how we found Him, when we came back—
Sitting on a well, talking to a woman?
Yes, a woman, would you believe!
But that wasn't all!
A foreigner, she was—
And a bad lot, at that . . .
You'd have thought, really,
That He'd have known better—
Wouldn't you, lads?

Then He was always round at Lazarus' place.
He seemed to like it there, somehow.
Remember how we found Him
Talking to those two sisters—
Martha and Mary?
There He sat, talking to the younger one
As though she were a man,
Instead of sending her off to the kitchen
To help that sharp-tongued sister of hers.
Anyone knows a woman's mind
Isn't built to take in that kind of teaching.
You'd think He'd have known that—
Wouldn't you, lads?

Then there was that woman
Who poured all that pricey ointment
Over His feet that day.
Actually wiped it off with her hair, she did!
I ask you—wouldn't you have thought He'd see
How that would make the tongues wag?
And He could so easily have sent her packing—
Couldn't He, lads?

And now here are these jabbering women—
The two Mary's, Joanna and the rest—
With some wild tale of having seen angels in the empty
    tomb!
As if Joseph of Arimathea
Hadn't laid the dear Body in the tomb himself
And seen it sealed!
Be quiet, you foolish women,
And stop these idle tales!
Things are bad enough as they are
Without your hysteria . . .

All the same, maybe I'll just slip round
To the garden, and see if everything's all right . . .
Coming, lads?

8

The Inner Man— or Woman

When one is forced to spend long periods of time in a hospital ward, whether as a patient, a nurse, or simply as a visitor, one cannot help observing many things about human nature which one might otherwise never learn. A nurse, for example, soon learns that women are, on the whole, more finicky about their food than men are! She observes, too, that men will often do anything to prolong their stay in hospital—in order, apparently, that they may continue to enjoy the ministration of gentle hands and feminine graces! Children, she finds, are by far the easiest of patients. On the whole, they make less fuss about their ailments, and will put up with much discomfort with very little complaint. Children accept, without question, much that life brings to them, but it is often the building up of inner protest, resentment, or fear based on experience and knowledge which increases the suffering of the average adult. When these elements are conquered and give place to acceptance, trust, and faith in a higher power, the sufferer then appears to be able to bear an astonishing amount of discomfort, and often amazes those who observe him.

One of the things which I learned—especially during the long hours spent in children's wards—was the noticeable difference in the way men and women carried their sorrow or anxiety over their sick children. Kim's parents were, perhaps, typical of this. Kim was a little girl of about three years old who, without any previous warning, had fallen down indoors while playing with her toys, and had lost consciousness. The time I first saw her, she had been in a coma for several weeks. Her mother used to come every day and sit by the bed of her little girl, talking to the doll-like figure in soft tones, begging her to wake up. She told me that she believed something of her own strong faith must communicate itself to the child, even in her unconsciousness, and that she would one day recover. I was deeply moved by the calm, unfailing devotion of this woman whose precious only child seemed to be so far beyond her reach.

Once, her husband came to visit his little daughter. Kim's mother had already told me that she had great difficulty in persuading him to come to the ward, because the prospect of doing so filled him with such dread. On this one occasion, he stayed for a few minutes only, forcing himself to look into the cot, then turned away with stark grief distorting the features of his big, manly face. My own heart was torn by the sight of his mute agony, the more so because this spectacle of male reaction in the face of suffering was becoming disturbingly familiar.

Can it be, I wondered, that suffering is a kind of second nature to the true woman? Throughout the ages she has been inured to it, bringing forth her children in soon forgotten travail, living out her life on the stormy seas of the emotions, weathering, in the very fibres of her being, hardship and poverty, disappointment, disillusionment and grief, cruelty and war, anxiety and loneliness of spirit. In a man's world, where action has never been her *forte*, it is inevitable that she must be the more vulnerable of the sexes. This is why true men have always sought to protect her. Yet throughout the ages, women have always been slighted, scorned, and often misunderstood, seldom finding a voice to express what lies in their innermost being. As Joyce Cary, the novelist, said of one of his characters: 'It seemed to him once more that women are a race apart in a world of which the fantastic difference is hidden only by their logical inability to detect and describe it . . .'

It is surely the passivity of woman which makes her what she is. She is the bearer of life: man must keep the wheels turning. He is concerned with shape and function—she with texture and colour. Since the beginning of time, this has been the order of things. Man is ruled by his head, woman by her heart. So that when man finds himself in a situation where rationalism or action are not only unnecessary, but futile, he is driven hard against an alien wall of inexpressible emotion. The only possible escape route is one of retreat.

This is what the disciples did at Calvary. One by one they forsook Him and fled, for they could not face the ultimate tragedy. But the grief-stricken women followed Him to the very end. Jesus Himself was fully aware of this, and He understood the very heart of womanhood. In the midst of

His own suffering, when the bitter cup was raised to His very lips. He could turn with selfless compassion to those following women and say: 'Daughters of Jerusalem, weep not for me but for yourselves and your children . . .'

But Jesus too, understood the heart of man—for He Himself was a man. We do not read that He reproached the runaway disciples when He met them again after His resurrection. He understood the agony in a man's heart when he is confronted with a situation where his physical strength is of no avail—for He knew what was in man. And that aggressive, protective element in a man's nature is perhaps frustrated most severely in the face of sorrow or grief.

George Eliot, describing the reaction of Tom and Maggie Tulliver to their father's financial failure in *The Mill on the Floss*, describes how they stood with beating heart to see how the sick man would take the shock of seeing, for the first time, his own home stripped bare of everything which had been sold up to pay his creditors.

'Of the two young hearts,' writes George Eliot, 'Tom suffered the most unmixed pain, for Maggie, with all her keen susceptibility, yet felt as if sorrow made larger room for her love to flow in, and gave breathing-space to her passionate nature. No true boy feels that; he would rather go and slay the Nemean lion, or perform any round of heroic labours than endure perpetual appeals to his pity for evils over which he can make no conquest.'

It seems to me that George Eliot, with her usual keen perception, goes to the heart of the matter here. For this, surely is the fundamental difference between men and women. When I hear modern women talking about the 'equality' of the sexes, I wonder what they mean. God has made the sexes to perfectly complement and balance each other, and the whole of civilization is in peril when we try to change the divine order of things. It is man whom God has appointed to be the 'manager' of life's affairs: authority is vested in him. But woman has an equally responsible role to fulfil, for she is the very heart of life. She has been described as 'the adorner of life, the civilizer', 'patroness of beauty and tranquillity', the 'creator of a sanctuary of love and delight in her home'. Women have always had a tremendous power of influence over those who love them, and the weight of their responsibility lies in the fact that this can be an influence for good or for evil.

Those women who shake their fists at the world of men and demand 'equality' are in fact, the very ones who believe that the male role is a superior one. This is shown clearly by those who imply by their behaviour that any job which is by tradition a 'man's job' must be a superior one to any that has been regarded in the past as 'woman's work'. This was illustrated recently by an American nurse who boasted that she was giving up her career to become a lorry-driver!

Now it seems to me that this is 'equality' gone mad! The militant supporters of so-called Women's Liberation are really suffering from a giant-sized inferiority complex. This, I believe, has been brought about in two ways.

I suppose it is true to say that, due to their dominant role in life, men have always looked down upon women. Dr Graham Howe says: 'Self surrender is the nature of the feminine principle. Therefore it may have suffered contempt during the passing of the centuries as being evidence of weakness. The feminine principle has always suffered the risk of shame, contempt and destruction, and it has always been unsafe to be a woman.'

In a bygone age, men saw to it that women knew very little about basic male attitudes; I suppose it was another way of 'protecting' womankind. The conversations in the barrack room, the public bar, and any other place from which female company was excluded, never reached the ears of women. Therefore they remained comparatively ignorant of the disdain which men felt (or, in the cause of male prestige, pretended to feel) for women in general. But the advent of the popular 'realistic' novel, the motion picture, and, in recent years, television and radio, changed all that. Through the medium of simulated reality, all secrets are uncovered. Derogatory remarks and generalizations about women are made public every day. Instead of being proud of their womanhood, women are beginning to be ashamed of it.

The other cause, I believe, for the 'uprising' of women is that our society has become obsessed and saturated with the subject of sex. Wherever one goes, woman is publicly depicted as an object by which man may satisfy his natural appetites. I say 'publicly' because this carnal view of woman, like the attitude previously mentioned, was once confined to the conclaves of all-male company. Now, nobody is able to escape from it. The heart of true womanhood will always cry out against the lie which proclaims that this is her chief *raison d'être*, and it is because of this obsession with loveless sex that modern woman feels degraded, depersonalized, and above all, *inferior*. 'Is this all I am?' she asks herself, 'Is this all they want of me?' Small wonder, to my mind, that many are forsaking and disowning a role which has been so besmirched and downgraded.

If the sanity of our human race is to be preserved, it seems essential that there should be a re-assessment of the true role of woman—the noble, exalted role which God first designed for her. 'It will be the task of the psychology of the whole man,' says Dr Howe, 'to re-establish the psychology of woman in her role of mediator, and not as satisfier of man's or child's needs. . . . Before, during and after being a mother, which is only a transient and relatively animal function, and as such is biologically catered for, woman is *woman* . . . She truly joins all parts of our world together by *being* woman, not by *doing* mother.'

It seems to me of great significance that Jesus Christ, the Son of God came to exalt what is usually described as the 'feminine principle'. His was a life of self-giving, sacrifice and shame. He was 'meek and lowly in heart'; He had compassion on the multitudes; He wept at the graveside of a friend; He turned the other cheek, and He condemned those who take the sword. Yet all these qualities have been labelled 'feminine' and scorned by strong men down the ages. Jesus had a strong, virile personality. His whole bearing spoke of manly authority. Yet where, in the gospels, is there any suggestion that Jesus rated physical courage above moral courage? All His severest condemnation was poured upon the Scribes and Pharisees for their arrogance and their hypocrisy. He spoke out fearlessly against the so-called 'male principles' of aggression, competitiveness, and gratification of the ego. Yet to the many women with whom He had personal dealings, He showed nothing but gentleness, honour, and patient understanding.

It is almost a cliché to say that 'Jesus honoured womanhood'. But if it is true, then does not this call for an approach to womanhood which for centuries has been patently lacking? Should not women be proud not only of the role with which God has entrusted them, but of the essential nature

99

which is theirs—and which will be lost if they make the mistake of trying to become like men? One shudders to think of a lop-sided, masculine world in which aggression, ambition and a reaching after personal and material success hold sway: a world where true women will feel ashamed to make home-building their chief interest, and where children will grow up without the love, security, warmth and character-training that only a mother can give. How is it that we have come to believe that the making of money is more important than the making of people? That a top executive job in this technological age is a far more worthy calling than that of a true woman in any walk of life?

Monica Furlong says that 'If Christianity is to have any life henceforward, then it seems likely that some rediscovery of the feminine will be necessary, in both men and women. We live in a world that has come to despise the feminine, which has only wistful dreams of beauty allied to goodness, and of generous comfort and giving.'

Surely there is something drastically wrong with an order of civilization where it is considered 'manly' (and therefore admirable) to drink, to swear, to make bawdy jokes, to indulge the fleshy appetites, and to laugh at religion. Conversely it is 'womanish' (and therefore laughable) to refrain from doing these things, or to condemn them in others. Is it to be wondered at that women have, during the last fifty years or so, rushed to climb aboard the masculine bandwaggon? Or any wonder that society has gone rotten at the core because of it?

Taylor Caldwell says that 'the decay and the ruin of a nation always has lain in the hands of its women. So does its life and strength, its reverence for beauty, its mercy, and kindness. And above all, its men.' The German poet Goethe said that 'the eternal feminine draws us upwards'. Yet to be feminine is still, in the minds of men and women alike, to be inferior.

The time has surely come for women to take a fresh look at themselves, and to see themselves as God intended them to be; and for men to stop guarding so jealously their 'superiority' and to concentrate on being the true leaders of mankind. Women want, more than ever, to be able to look up to their men—not simply because they are *men*, but because they are noble, and know what is good and right.

Often, when I am in conversation with a young wife after

a meeting of some kind, she will say to me: 'I'm interested in Christian things—I want to know more. My neighbour brought me along tonight. I know she has something I don't have in my life, and I want it for myself. But my husband—he just doesn't want to know. He hates me even to talk about it. He shuts up like a clam and won't even tell me what he thinks. He doesn't mind me going to church, but he won't come. I don't want to cause a division in the family. What can I do? Because I can see that before long it's going to come between us.'

Why are our men afraid to face up to spiritual claims? Why do they turn their backs on the Church, when they should be taking their places, as heads of their families, in the ranks of those who fight for truth and righteousness? Is it because committal to Christ involves a passive acceptance, a surrender which is foreign to the male nature? If action were what was called for, might not matters be different? Monica Furlong in her book *The Journey In*, has this to say:

'Our problem is not that we take refuge from action in spiritual things, but that we take refuge from spiritual things in action . . . we dread the pain of self-discovery . . . Keep going, pitiful ghosts of real people that we are—that is the message. The real leaders in the coming years will be those who sabotage this effort—those who know that the road to action lies through holiness and wholeness.'

The inner man cries out for wholeness—and so does the inner woman. But man will never be whole until he looks to the perfect man, Jesus Christ, for an example, till he learns to absorb within his masculinity the 'feminine' principle of self-giving; and woman will never be whole until she is able, once more to respect her own femininity, and know herself to be safely enfolded in masculine authority and moral strength.

Father in Heaven,
Giver of every good and perfect gift,
I praise You this day for the glory of Your creation,
For the beauty, and the intricacy and perfection of its pat-
tern.
For the changing seasons, which remind us of Your faith-
fulness;
For the beauty of trees in winter,
For the miracle of new, green life in spring,
For the golden days of summer,
And for the mellow fruitfulness of autumn.
Lord, You could have made our world black and white,
With just those things necessary for the maintenance of
life,
But You did not.
You gave us a multicoloured world, with a glorious variety
of texture and shape and substance.
You gave us running rivers and roaring seas, soaring moun-
tains and rolling plains; dense green forests and the
minute perfection of a myriad flowers;
Fish and fowl and insect, and the whole animal kingdom to
delight us and inspire us . . .
And then, Lord, You made man—the crown and glory of
Your creation.
Fearfully and wonderfully was he made,
Male and female created You them,
With strength of mind and muscle for the man
And tenderness, warmth and beauty for the woman.
So perfectly did they complement each other,
With all the different parts blending and merging,
To make MAN, *a creature fashioned in Your likeness.*
Lord, forgive us, if we have failed
In the holy role You created for us to fulfil,
The divine purpose You set before us.
Forgive us if we have ever scorned or derided
The role or the nature of ourself or of the other;
Or if we have ever been ashamed or resentful
Of our appointed lot.
And although sin has spoilt Your pattern,
Mixing lust with love,
And tears with toil,
And pain with pleasure,
Thus marring the perfection of Your design,

Nevertheless, help us each day perfectly to fulfil
The high calling, the stern responsibility
With which You have entrusted us.
May we be Your men
And Your women—
Unashamed and unafraid:
For the future of our world depends upon it,
Father, Creator of life and order.
May we never forget this.
For Your dear Son's sake.

Amen

The Beginning of Wisdom

For him that seeketh
  No ground is barren ground.
No search is fruitless,
  Though treasure be not found:
For often those that we call wasted years
Have yielded richness—wisdom born of tears.

For him that learneth
  Nothing is truly known
Until he seeth
  Beyond the vision shown:
For every truth is a transparency
Through which another truth gleams distantly.

Where, then, is wisdom?
  He knoweth most who knows
That he knows nothing:
  The seed of wisdom grows
Within the silent man whose ears have heard
The glorious death-cry of the Living Word.

9
The Inner Eye

Another 'feminine' principle which has come in for a certain amount of disrespect in this materialistic age is that of human creativity. In recent years, the arts have taken second place to the sciences, so that knowledge, the accumulation of facts, and technical skill have superseded wisdom, truth, and the quest for beauty. It is fashionable to speak with thinly veiled contempt about poetry, painting and serious music. So-called 'manly' pursuits, such as sport, physical exploits and scientific developments are the preoccupations of today. This downgrading of the arts is surely yet another symptom of our modern age; of the insidious disease which is eating at the vitals of our civilization. *For where there is no vision, the people perish.*

'Vision' is truth received through the 'inner eye' of man—a reaching out of the finite mind toward the infinite. Spiritual truth cannot be received through the intellect alone. In the arts we see man groping toward this 'vision', and then striving to express through his own chosen medium something of what he has seen with his inner eye.

'The cistern contains,' said William Blake, 'the fountain overflows.' This may be said to illustrate the essential difference between the scientific and the creative mind. The one can contain his knowledge, the other cannot. The creative artist is under a compulsion to express what he knows, or feels he knows, the academic stores his knowledge away. Furthermore, there is a basic difference between the kind of knowledge accumulated by the scholar and the artist. For the scholar absorbs knowledge chiefly through his intellect, while the artist receives it through the finer instincts and the imagination too—his inner eye. In the Bible we find that divine revelation is transmitted by means of a perfect balance of academic and poetic writing; but, as we shall see later, the strongest appeal is made to the inner eye. The modern mind is filled with a dreary collection of disjointed facts, and half-formed ideas culled from quick and easy application to the mass media. Small wonder that we are a shallow-thinking, uncreative, colourless generation. We have forgotten how to bring all our God-given faculties into use in our accumulation of knowledge. We know, but we do not understand. We are a people bereft of wisdom.

Rebecca West wrote a novel and used Blake's observation for the epigraph. From this she extracted her title: *The Fountain Overflows*. It is a story about a family for whom music is the real world, and everything else is irrelevant. Music is shown throughout the book to be a symbol of order and serenity. It is Rose, the young and budding musician who differentiates between mere technical skill and knowledge, and creative 'vision'.

'When Mamma played,' related Rose, 'she was making clear something which the composer had found out and which nobody had known before him. It might even be that by the emphasis she placed on the different parts of his discovery, she could add something to it of which nobody, not even the composer, had before been conscious. In her playing there was a gospel and an evangelist who preached it, and that implied a church which worshipped a God not yet fully revealed but in the course of revelation. But when cousin Jock played, he created about him a world in which all was known, and in which art was not a discovery but a decoration. All then was trivial, and there was no meaning in art or life.'

The creative artist, then, not only expresses what he knows, nor even what he feels to be true: he presents to the world a peculiar vision of knowledge which is on the periphery of his own comprehension. For the musician this 'other world' of knowledge comes to him through sounds; for the artist, it is expressed in colour and form; for the writer, words and ideas are the medium, and for the sculptor it is shape and texture which mould the raw stone into a living thing.

A little later on in Rebecca West's story, we hear Mary talking to her sister:

' "What is music about?" I asked.
' "Oh, it is about life, I suppose, and especially about the parts of life we do not understand, otherwise people would not have to worry about it by explaining it by music. But I can't say what I mean."

'What was music? I suddenly felt sick because I did not know the answer.'

Perhaps Mary summed up for us here the essence of all art. It is 'especially about the parts of life we do not understand'. If it were about aspects of life which could be easily explained and understood in terms of logic, then it would be irrelevant. But the artist takes us to the edge of human reason and shows us an infinity beyond which humbles us. This is how Rose felt when Mary tried to explain what music was 'about'. She felt suddenly sick because she realized how limited her own understanding was. This is the effect that true art should have on the observer; it should awaken in him the awareness of a realm of truth beyond his comprehension.

Those of us who express impatience with any painting, for example, which does not present objects and people in a form that we can readily understand, are perhaps showing that we do not appreciate the real purpose of art. The technical skill and knowledge required to produce a 'realistic' painting is very great, but the viewer may feel little more than admiration for the artist's craftsmanship, or appreciation of the beauty of the objects represented when he is confronted with the finished work. Such a picture, despite its academic perfection, is, to use Rose's words, not a 'discovery' but a 'decoration'. But a less conventional picture executed by a great painter such as Van Gogh or El Greco may call forth from the discerning viewer far more than this. The artist's own peculiar vision is there in the picture, but portrayed in dimensions which are outside normal conscious experience. By holding up a mirror to a world beyond our reach, the artist has awakened in us faculties and yearnings of which we may hitherto have been unaware. Or he has called forth in us chords which rarely vibrate, and which need the stimulus of other people's creativity to waken them to life. Our inner eye has been opened.

We have all experienced this kind of awakening in some form or another. We have looked at a picture and felt something indefinable stir within us, though when we try to analyse what it is that has called forth this response we cannot readily do so. Or we may read a poem which conveys no immediate meaning to our minds, yet evokes, somewhere deep within us some half-forgotten experience.

When I was in my teens I learned by heart the whole of Francis Thompson's long poem—*The Hound of Heaven*. I loved this poem not only for the picture it presented of a soul in flight from the pursuing love of God, but for the sheer beauty of its poetry. Even today the rich, yet delicate imagery is there like a fine lacing at the back of my memory, and I have only to reach back and I can touch any part of it. Each time I do this, the sheer beauty of the words takes my breath away as though I were hearing them for the first time:

> *I said to dawn, Be sudden; to eve, Be soon;*
> > *With thy young skiey blossoms heap me over*
> > > *From this tremendous Lover!*
> *Float thy vague veil about me, lest He see!*

Such exquisite beauty of expression defies analysis: we bow our heads before it, speechless.

Similarly, I can never listen to Beethoven's sixth symphony, the Pastoral, without being transported to the meadows of my childhood. It is as though all my senses are awakened at once. I can see the burnished gold of the buttercups leaning toward the morning sun; I can feel the tingling chill of the dew under my sandalled feet, and hear the haunting call of the cuckoo; I smell the pungency of the sun-warmed earth; almost I taste the sharpness of new air upon my lips. I am aware of the peculiar, pale green freshness of an early summer morning, and I find my heart soaring with an almost physical delight as I listen. The reason is that Beethoven has recreated from his own consciousness a spiritual experience, and invited me to share it. He has transmitted through the created sounds, the kind of beauty which can only be appreciated through the senses and the finer instincts. He has therefore elevated us temporarily above the materialism of our everyday lives.

One reviewer of my book *Beyond the Shadows* said that 'sometimes the poet in the writer takes too much hold on the style'. Yet in talking to the many readers to whom the book has been of special help, it is this very element in the writing which seems to have been of most value. The same reviewer began by saying, 'This book is more than a book—it is an experience.' This, in essence, is what is said by practically all who have read it, I believe that it is because of the God-given gift which enabled me to write 'creatively' that the book has been of such value. Many said: 'It is not just like reading an account of what happened to you: you invited me to share the experience with you. Once I began to read, I couldn't stop—I was completely carried away, and I felt it was all happening to me.'

Robert Liddell said that what we look for in literature is 'a lack of faith in simple or easy solutions to human problems, a sense of the frailty of life . . . no loud, hearty songs of innocence, but quiet songs of experience.' The poet, the painter, the musician, the novelist, the sculptor—each through his chosen medium—distills for us his own peculiar essence of reality which he has extracted from the heart of life. And we, tasting it, are enriched.

It is, perhaps, a rather sad reflection on many 'evangelical' Christians that they are often lacking in the kind of sensitivity which responds to the artist's vision of life. For the danger is that our own doctrinal 'certainty' makes us sing 'loud, hearty songs of innocence' instead of 'quiet songs of experience'. The trouble is that the 'innocence' often hides a lack of knowledge or understanding of the finer issues which trouble the minds of many outside the Church. In our eagerness to cry that 'Christ is the answer', we overlook the fact that Christ Himself never offered simple or easy solutions to human problems, and that much of His teaching is veiled in poetic language, not clothed in dogmatic phraseology.

When His disciples asked Jesus why He always spoke in parables, He replied: 'Because it is given unto you to know the mysteries of the kingdom of heaven, but to them it is not given.' Jesus uses a word here which many of us are afraid of—'mystery'. And He suggests that only those who are seeking the truth are able to perceive it. The word 'mystery' implies something which the finite mind can never fully understand. Paul spoke often of 'mystery'—the 'mystery which from the beginning has been hidden in God'. 'Now,' he said, 'we see in a glass, darkly, but then face to face.' We must be careful that, in our joy over the 'certainties' of the gospel, we do not lose that essential humility which every man must feel when he stands in the presence of truths far beyond the reach of the human mind. Although we believe that God has revealed the truth to us in His Son, we must also accept that the complete revelation of Himself cannot take place until we meet Him face to face, having shed the limitations of mortality. This is why Jesus used picture language constantly during His earthly ministry. There is a sense in which truth cannot be 'taught'; it has to be 'transmitted'—through the inner eye.

We can trace this method of communication right back into the Old Testament. The writings of the prophets are steeped in poetic language, and Isaiah 53 is a classic example of this. These books are full of rich imagery: there is hardly a verse which does not tell, in vivid pictorial language, what is in the mind of the holy God of Israel. Take this verse from Jeremiah's second chapter, for example:

> For my people have committed two evils;
> They have forsaken me, the fountain of living waters,
> And hewed them out cisterns,
> Broken cisterns, that can hold no water.

The impact of this statement goes straight to our hearts and our consciences: we do not need to stop and work out what is meant by 'fountains', 'living water' or 'broken cisterns'. We know.

The poetic books themselves—Psalms, Song of Songs, Job and Proverbs are peculiarly precious to us, and the reason why they mean so much more to us than the historical accounts of Jewish history, is that they are presented in a form we can readily assimilate. Why should this be—when they are obviously 'veiled' in poetic language, while the historical books are simple factual accounts? It is because the faculty which is brought into use when we read them is the inner eye.

When David sang: 'As the hart panteth after the waterbrooks, so pants my soul after thee, my God!' He was using poetic language because he knew that no other language could express what was in his heart. We do not need to work out what he meant: *we know*. Our inner eye sees the quivering hart, feels the parched dryness, tastes the cold brook water, and we cry: 'That is how much I need my God!'

Yet, with this rich literary heritage, the Jews still expected their Messiah to be a man of action, a warrior—not the teacher, poet, prophet that He was! But—'I am the Light of the world,' He said. 'I am the Bread of Life.' 'I am the Way, the Truth and the Life: no man cometh unto the Father but by Me.' He knew that, just as the child learns about the world in which he lives by looking at pictures, so we mortals can only learn of divine things through parables, through picture language, and through poetic thought.

Dr Howe has said: 'Truth is not a plain tale. It cannot be told simply, as if it were a straight line, with a beginning and an end, word for word, once and for all. It is too subtle, too manifold, and too self-contradictory for that. Like hunters after our prey, we can have a shot at it with a quick-fire of words, and when we miss, shoot at it again from a different direction. Then, either all our shots must miss, or even if we hit it we shall do injury to truth, merely wounding it by our injustice. Then we must try again, but more as poets do, to catch it in a picture, and see a fleeting glimpse of it as it disappears like water through a sieve. In truth, the truth cannot be caught nor held, nor simply told, because it is more subtle than the mind can see . . .'

Although we may agree in principle with what Dr Howe is saying, we must bear in mind that Jesus said: 'Ye shall know the truth and the truth shall make you free.' He *was* the Truth, and as partakers of the divine nature of Christ we can—and must—rejoice in specific Christian 'certainties'. But in the midst of our 'certainty', let us return again and again in deep humility of spirit to the verses with which John, poet and seer, begins his gospel:

> *In the beginning was the Word*
> *And the Word was with God*
> *And the Word was God.*
> *The same was in the beginning with God.*
> *All things were made by Him;*
> *And without Him was not anything made that was*
>   *made.*
> *In Him was life*
> *And the life was the light of men.*
> *And the light shineth in darkness;*
> *And the darkness comprehended it not.*

In the beginning was the Word, the *Logos*—the perfect expression of the invisible God . . . but let us not fall into the trap of trying to explain, to break it down into logical thought, or we shall destroy it. We simply bow before the exquisite word-picture, and receive, through our inner eye—the eye of faith—the Living Word Himself.

O, Lord eternal,
Who art the Way, the Truth and the Life;
The Living Word,
Creator of all things,
We bow before Thee now in humility of spirit.
Thou who art veiled in splendour and mystery,
Whose crown is the sun,
And whose sceptre is the stars,
Who wast, and art, and evermore shalt be;
The glory of whose face is so bright
That none may look upon Thee and live—
We prostrate ourselves before Thee
And we are speechless.
And yet, O Living Word,
Thou hast deigned to reveal Thyself to us,
Fallen, wretched creatures that we are.
Touch, with Thy burning ray,
Our poor dark minds.
Open our deaf ears
And our blind eyes
That we might receive
Thy meaning,
Thy mystery,
Thyself.
In poverty and humility we crave it, O King of the Universe:
For we are unworthy, unready, unclean . . .

            Amen

A Ballad of Life and Death

'Why should I die?' the dead man said.
  'Why should I lay down my life?'
(He didn't know he was dead, you see:
  No one does till he sees the knife.)

The Man with the knife said: 'Don't be afraid—
  There's nothing to kill but Death.'
'But I live! Can't you hear my beating heart
  And feel the warmth of my breath?'

'I hear the knocking of bone on bone
  As the skeleton struggles for life;
And I see the foul smoke from the pit of Death—
  Let me set you free with My knife!'

The dead man wavered. 'But sir,' he said,
  'Your knife is sharp and long;
And besides, if all that you say is true,
  And I am the one who is wrong'—

(For the man was just beginning to feel
  That whether he lived or no,
Any state, whatever it cost him now,
  Was better than this. And so—)

'If I'm really dead,' he said with a frown,
  'What good is your knife, good sir?'
'Do you want to live?' was the sudden demand.
  But the dead man did not stir.

'Do you want to live?' And the Strange Man's voice
  Was deeper and gentler now;
The man at His feet gave a weary sigh;
  He nodded, his hand on his brow.

Then, gently, over the lifeless breast
    The Stranger laid His heart.
'Take this knife, and pierce My heart and yours
    And bid cold Death depart.'

Then horror filled the dead man's face.
    'But I cannot take your life!'
'Do you think I would ask you to die alone?
    Obey Me: You have the knife.'

The dead man shuddered and closed his eyes.
    Then, over the Strange Man's breast,
He raised the knife and brought it down
    Till in his own heart it was pressed.

He felt no pain, for his heart was stone,
    But he knew that Death was dead.
For into his veins from the Strange Man's breast
    The blood flowed warm and red.

He withdrew the knife, and the Stranger rose
    And helped him from the ground.
But the man cried out when he saw the blood
    That flowed from the other's wound.

The Stranger smiled and took his hand.
    'You had no blood to shed!
But now you have, for you share My life
    And can never die,' He said.

10
The Inner Certainty

Perhaps the most common remark made to me by readers of
Beyond the Shadows is one regarding the question of faith.
Many say: 'I wish I had your faith!' or, 'Of course, I do not
have a faith like yours, but . . .' These comments are usually
made by people who are not committed Christians, but
sometimes a Christian will say impulsively: 'I'm afraid my
faith would never stand that kind of test!'

This has led me to examine the whole vital question
of faith in Jesus Christ. For often, when non-Christians speak
so wistfully—or, as is sometimes the case, so defen-
sively—about their lack of faith, I am at a loss to know
just how to answer them in the brief encounters during
which such remarks are often made. In my heart, the answer
is there: 'What you need is not my faith, but my Saviour!'
But, rightly or wrongly, I am always hesitant about saying
this kind of thing to a complete stranger. After all, I do not
really know what their spiritual experience—if any—might
be: I can only surmise it from the kind of remark they
make.

What does disturb me is the complimentary tone of voice
in which the remark is nearly always made—as if I had
achieved great heights in the exercise of faith; as if, in fact,
credit were somehow due to me for having come through
the experiences described in my story. Sometimes I hasten to
say that faith is a gift, not something to be achieved by
effort. Sometimes I say that in the experience itself I learned
just how irrelevant my own faith, or lack of it, really were;
that the victory which my husband and I tasted was all of
grace; that it came to us *in spite of* ourselves, *in spite of* our
weakness.

'But how does this work? How can I find a faith like this?
What is lacking in me?' is the puzzled response. Some may
be good at explaining these mysteries to others in a few
concise, telling phrases, with ample illustrations from Scrip-
ture. For my own part, I am glad of an opportunity to work
out my answer on paper, and pray that what I shall say

about this vital subject may throw light on it for some who still feel that they have questions to ask.

First of all, what is faith? The Victorian writer and novelist, George Macdonald has this to say: 'Do you ask, "What is faith in Him?" I answer, The leaving of your way, your objects, your self, and the taking of His and Him; the leaving of your trust in men, in money, in opinion, in character . . . and *doing as He tells you*. I can find no words strong enough to serve for the weight of this obedience.'

Many people never discover what faith really is, because they have never experienced this initial abandonment. They have never recognized their own need, never let go of their own independence, never asked Christ to cleanse and renew them and to take over their lives.

In another of George Macdonald's books, the allegorical story entitled *The Golden Key*, he writes:

'The Old Man of the Earth stooped over the floor of the cave, raised a huge stone, and left it leaning. It disclosed a great hole that went plumb-down. "That is the way," he said. "But there are no stairs. You must throw yourself in. There is no other way." '

Human nature does not find it easy to throw itself into the unknown. We crave for stairs, for steps to lead us safely on. We beg to be allowed to understand how it is that the death of a man two thousand years ago can have any bearing on our own individual needs today. When we begin to reason out the teaching of the New Testament, to translate into logical thought the doctrine that Christ was bearing in His body on the cross our sins; that His death atones for the sins of all who put their trust in Him, and that His resurrection has secured for us eternal life, our minds boggle. We cry, as Mary did to Gabriel: 'How can this be?' We beg to be led, by steps of reason and logic, into the unknown realms of faith.

But Paul said: 'By grace are ye saved, through faith, and that not of yourselves, lest any man should boast. It is the gift of God.' Faith is a gift, but like any other gift, it has to be accepted. Faith is both a decisive act and a sustained attitude. In other words, it begins by a conscious abandonment of self-reliance, and a transfer of our dependence to Jesus Christ, and to the truths expressed in His Word.

The will, then, is involved in this initial grasp of faith, for often those who say sadly, 'I would like to believe, but I cannot. I have too many intellectual objections,' are really saying: 'I am not willing to abandon my own sufficiency, my own way of seeing things. I am not willing to admit that I need a Saviour from sin.'

Abandonment, therefore, is the name of the key which opens the door to faith. Abandonment of self-sufficiency, self-esteem and self-will. Abandonment, in fact, of the whole self. When this has taken place—and not until then—faith begins to grow. It is a new birth.

After this initial decisive act, then we find that our faith rests on certain facts which are clearly set out in the New Testament. These are the facts, already mentioned, of what Christ has done for us. He is the Son of God, Who gave Himself for us, dying for our sins on the cross. He was buried, and rose again from the dead, thus procuring for us forgiveness of sins and eternal life. These, basically, are the simple facts upon which our faith rests.

But our faith moves beyond the facts to trusting a *Person*, when we take a *personal* stand upon the facts themselves. In other words, as soon as we acknowledge that Christ came to save the individual that is 'I', then we establish a personal relationship with Him. We put our trust entirely upon the Person, Jesus Christ; not merely upon the facts concerning Him. Until we understand this, we shall never know anything about the life of faith, because not until we are linked eternally with God in Jesus Christ does faith become a habit, a sustained attitude of heart and mind. This is why faith is described as one of the fruits of the Spirit: It is a natural outcome of being linked with God, of being indwelt by His Spirit.

This is something which I did not perfectly understand, until after the experience of trial and testing through which my husband and I passed in the illness and loss of our daughter. Readers of the book will recall how, shortly before the blow fell, I had been doing a lot of heart-searching. I was asking myself that very question which other Christians have asked themselves since reading the story: 'How would I make out if my faith was put to the test?' And often I would answer, as so many other self-questioners have answered: 'I'm sure my faith would not be strong enough—I'm not made of the right kind of stuff.' But I had overlooked the fact that faith, like peace and joy, is a fruit of the Spirit. Faith grows naturally in the heart of the one who is rooted in the living Christ.

So that when the time came, and I cried, 'Why, Lord, why?' faith answered: *'Trust Me.'* And when we prayed for healing, believing that the touch of Christ had 'still its ancient power', faith answered once more, simply: *'Trust Me.'* And when Frankie asked us why Jesus did not answer her prayers and make her better, we turned, like children to Him for an answer. It came: *'Trust Me.'* When later we watched her die, stood helplessly by and saw her suffer, I felt deep within me a despair so terrible, that momentarily, I let go of Him. My heart cried: 'There's nothing, there's nobody, no sense in this or in any of life . . .'

When I was interviewed for a B.B.C. radio programme on the day that the book was published, I was asked whether at any time my faith gave way. I replied by describing how I had, momentarily let go of God; and how, in that dark moment, it was if He said: 'Trust Me; you may let go of Me, but I will never let go of you.' When the interview was actually broadcast, part of it had been cut out for the sake of time, so listeners never heard me say that I believed the essence of faith to be expressed in the words of Job: 'Though He slay me, yet will I trust Him.' I was sorry this had to be omitted, for it might have helped some questioning soul to an understanding of what faith is really about. Faith trusts where it cannot see, walks with confidence in the darkness, because it is founded upon a Person—the omnipotent, omniscient, all-loving Son of God Himself. Furthermore, it goes on trusting when everything around cries out against the madness of such a trust.

If, when you were a child, your father had asked you to wait in a certain spot while he went off on an errand, and if he assured you that he would be back for you, you would not doubt for a moment that he would come back. No matter how long he was gone, still you would not worry about his intention to return to you, because he had promised to do so, and therefore you knew he would. He was your father, and you loved and trusted him. He had never let you down, and you knew that he never would. What is more, if he did not come back for you, would you not still go on trusting him? There must be some explanation, you would assert. You knew your father too well to doubt him.

How much more can we put our trust entirely in a heavenly Father? Even though there may be things He has not explained to us, even though there are things we do not understand, even though at times, it seems that He has forsaken us completely, yet faith, that ever-living, ever growing fruit within us, can never be destroyed. It will go on living and growing and—wonder of wonders—will be fertilized and enriched by suffering and trial. Because we are *in Him*.

Peter says that the 'trial of your faith' is 'much more precious than of gold that perishes' and he tells us to rejoice when our faith is tested in this way. Gold, when it is 'tried in the fire' becomes purer, brighter, more precious; and so it is with our faith. It is not for nothing that He asks His children to suffer, and it is not for nothing that He asks them to watch their loved ones suffer, hard though this may be to accept. For it is in these moments that He tests our self-abandonment. Suffering burns away everything except the core of our innermost being; but when this is clothed in the golden armour of faith, it only shines the more brightly.

The soul who refuses to abandon himself to Christ, the soul who clings tenaciously to his sufficiency will find that he has no resources with which to meet the storms of life. Jesus told the parable of the two houses to illustrate this point. The house which was built on the sand crumbled and fell when the wind and the rains came, while the house on the rock stood firm. Our self-sufficiency is like sand—comfortable and good to look at, but no good at all as a foundation for life. The rock, though hard and rugged, will never move, come what may.

Not long after I had finished writing *Beyond the Shadows*, I was put in touch with the mother of a little boy suffering from leukaemia. I was told that this woman was a professing Christian, but that she was very much in need of help, as she was 'losing her faith'. I corresponded with this distraught sufferer over many months, trying to pass on to her something of what we ourselves had experienced in similar circumstances. She, as we had done, was trusting God for a miracle to save her little boy, but as she watched him gradually deteriorating—not just over one year, as we had done, but for several—she became bitter and resentful. Why, she wanted to know, when God had promised to give us anything that we ask for in Christ's name, should He deny her such a simple thing as the life of her precious child?

I knew, of course, as any mother would, just how she felt. My heart suffered with her as she sent me periodic reports of her son's 'progress'. But I was deeply saddened when she wrote of wanting nothing to do with a God 'who did not keep His promises'. What had happened to her 'faith'?

I do not believe that anyone who has once received the gift of faith from God through the death of His Son Jesus Christ, can ever lose it, and I always question, when people speak of having lost their 'faith' whether they ever really possessed the real thing, or only a spurious substitute for it. When I asked the mother in this particular tragedy to tell me how she first became a Christian, she replied that she had just 'drifted' into it, and that she had never really felt close to God until her son was taken ill and she really needed Him. I then suggested to her that her present mental agony was due to the fact that she had never truly committed herself to Christ, never abandoned her will to Him in that vital initial step to faith. She admitted that this was true, and wrote later to say that she had still not been able to surrender her will to God. Quite honestly, she added, what is there to look forward to in this complete surrender? If we leave everything in God's hands and it appears to be His wish to make us miserable and unhappy, it hardly seems worth it!

The basis of this poor woman's complaint was that she had put her trust in God, had exercised faith in Him, but that He had failed her. He had let her down. What she really meant was that she had trusted Him to give her something which she felt His word clearly promised—i.e., physical healing for her child—and because this was denied her, she felt cheated. This is not faith, understandable though it may be from the point of view of any loving, suffering parent. And I cannot help adding that since our own experience, we have become very cautious about the whole question of physical healing, since we have seen so much harm done by those who insist that healing must be God's will every time, and that where this is not forthcoming, there must be a 'lack of faith' on the part of the person concerned. The young mother mentioned above was the victim of just such an emphasis. Those who hold these views have imperfectly understood the meaning of the gift of faith. Faith causes us to put our trust in the *Person* of Christ, not merely in what He can do for us.

Paradoxically (or so it might seem) the story of this unhappy woman did not end in despair or hopelessness. Although her little boy died, she was able to write afterwards of a sense of great upholding which came to her and her husband at the end. She realized now, said this mother, that her son had received a more complete and lasting healing than ever could have been given on earth. 'Although we had prayed for three years and eight months for healing on earth, our prayers were answered beyond our dreams.' Her precious child, she told me, was now with his Maker—that God in Whom she had often said she could no longer believe. What had happened to cause such a change of heart? Perhaps, as a result of the many prayers which had been offered up to God on her behalf, she heard the Voice which Francis Thompson the poet records, saying to her, out of His great heart of love:

> All which I took from thee I did but take
> Not for thy harms
> But just that thou mightst seek it in My arms;
> All which thy child's mistake
> Fancies as lost, I have stored for thee at home:
> Rise, clasp My hand and come!
> Halts by me that footfall:
> Is my gloom after all,
> Shade of His hand outstretched caressingly?
> 'Ah, fondest, blindest, weakest,
> I am He whom thou seekest!
> Thou dravest love from thee, who dravest Me.'

Paul said: 'I am crucified with Christ: nevertheless, I live; yet not I, but Christ liveth in me: and the life which I now live in the flesh, I live by the faith of the Son of God, who loved me and gave Himself for me'. *Not I but Christ* . . . This is the wonder of the life of faith. Not my *faith*, but my *Saviour* is what I commend to all those who are buffeted by life, or by the fear of what life may bring. And although faith is only one of the many gifts He imparts to us through His Spirit, yet in a sense it is the greatest of them all, because it forms the basis, the foundation of our very lives. It is through faith that we are able to say: 'Though He slay me, yet will I trust Him.' It is through faith that we are able to enjoy peace with God, and peace in all the complex circumstances of life; through faith we are able to know joy in our hearts at all times, and through faith we have hope for the future; through faith we are able to overcome temptation, witness to others, dare the impossible for God, and face death without fear.

Jesus said that faith can move mountains, and men and women have proved this over and over through the ages. What was it that made Gladys Aylward, a tiny cockney housemaid from London, travel alone to China via Russia and Japan—never having been further than the Isle of Wight in her life before—and face terrifying perils which would have shaken a trained soldier? Simply a God-given faith that He was calling her to missionary work among China's needy millions. As she sat by the railway line in complete darkness and bitter cold, somewhere in the wilds of Russia, boiling water in her tin kettle in order to make herself a drink of Oxo, she heard the wolves barking not far away. Alone, amid unknown dangers, in an alien land, she clung to the one certainty left to her: God had called her, and He would see her through.

When, years later in China, a riot broke out in the local jail, the prison officers were terrified. A prisoner had gone berserk and had a knife. One man had already been killed, blood flowed on the prison floor and all was mad, screaming confusion. Who was sent for to quell the riot? None other than Gladys Aylward, the small woman, as she was affectionately called. 'You say you have faith in your God—that He is a God who is alive—so get in there and stop the butchery!' What could she say? She staked all on the one who had saved and commissioned her. She marched into the jail and ordered the prisoners to be quiet. 'Give me that knife!' she commanded the half-crazed murderer. And meekly, he did.

Faith takes the weakest, the smallest, the most timid, and makes him into a giant. Because faith is the link that joins us to the infinite, the source of all strength. Never let the Christian say: 'My faith would not stand the test,' as though faith were a link attached to him and to nothing else. The man who doubts his faith is doubting his Saviour. The man who questions his ability to do anything is doubting the greatness of his God.

And let not the man who is yet uncommitted to Christ say wistfully: 'I wish I had a faith like that'—as though somehow he has been denied a blessing freely given to others. 'Come unto Me,' says Christ. It is a universal cry, a universal invitation. But He waits for an answer from your inside room.

O Great Eternal God,
Three in One,
Creator of the Universe,
Saviour of mankind,
And indwelling, all-pervading Holy Spirit,
Almost it seems presumptuous to say it—
But I abandon myself, in this moment,
Completely to You.
I abandon my self-sufficiency,
For I am hopeless, I am helpless, lost,
A soul in bondage to self and sin.
I abandon my self-esteem,
For I am nothing, I am nobody, of no consequence,
And all my righteousnesses are as filthy rags in Your sight.
I abandon my self-will,
For I am disobedient, proud, rebellious,
And like a sheep I have gone astray.
I abandon myself,
For I am nothing, I know nothing, can say nothing
That is of any value or significance:
But for what I am worth, Lord,
Here I am.
I surrender myself, the inner core of my being
To You, Lord of heaven and earth.
And in simple faith
I leave the rest to You.
For—can it be true?—
You have redeemed me,
You have bought me, poor thing that I am,
With Your precious blood.
So I lie, a poor naked thing in the palm of Your hand,
A soul reborn,
A new creation,
Ready, O Lord of Life,
To be clothed in Your righteousness,
And Your beauty.
Ready
For a life of joy and victory and purpose.

For You have set me down, now,
On the very edge of Eternity;
And I am gloriously, triumphantly, thankfully,
Alive—for ever.

And Thine is the Kingdom
The power
And the glory
For ever and ever,
World without end,

Amen